WISDOM OF TAROT

<u>Rosicrucian Order of the Golden Dawn Publications</u>

<u>The Golden Dawn Alchemy Series</u>

The Secret Fire – An Alchemical Study
By E.J. Langford Garstin

Hermetic Alchemy – Science and Practice
By Paul Foster Case

<u>The Golden Dawn Tarot Series</u>

Wisdom of Tarot
By Paul Foster Case

Tarot Revelations
By Paul Foster Case

Additional titles planned for both of these series

Please check www.rogd.org/books for latest update

Wisdom of Tarot

By Paul Foster Case

"Our Matter has as many names as there are things in this world;
that is why the foolish know it not."

First Published in 1931 as
'Tarot Instruction, Section First' by
THE SCHOOL OF AGELESS WISDOM
279 Newbury Street, Boston, Mass.

2009

Rosicrucian Order of the Golden Dawn

www.rogd.org

It is with great excitement that we introduce the first volume of the 'The Golden Dawn Tarot Series', a collection of distinguished books on Tarot written by leaders of the Golden Dawn Tradition.

The first book of this series, 'Wisdom of Tarot', represents some of Paul Foster Case's earliest thoughts on the subject. Though almost two decades will pass before the publication of Paul's masterpiece, 'The Tarot, A Key to the Wisdom of the Ages', all of his essential thought can be found in these pages as well as additional material that has not been available to the public for over 75 years.

This book, and its more advanced companion, 'Tarot Revelations', were originally distributed as 'Tarot Instruction, Section First' and 'Tarot Instruction, Section Second'. These texts followed Sections A, B, C, and D and came before the 'Hermetic Alchemy: Science and Practice' course in the original 'School of Ageless Wisdom' course curriculum. Sections A, B, C, and D were recently published as 'The Early Writings, Volume 1 and 2' by the Fraternity of the Hidden Light; 'Hermetic Alchemy: Science and Practice' was recently published by the Rosicrucian Order of the Golden Dawn as the second volume in the 'The Golden Dawn Alchemy' series.

With the publication of these texts, the entire course curriculum of Paul Foster Case, as distributed by the School of Ageless Wisdom, is now available to students of the Golden Dawn Tradition.

Enjoy!

Tony DeLuce
Laguna Niguel, CA
June 1st, 2009

THE OBJECT OF TAROT PRACTICE

If you will stop for a moment and consider the chain of circumstances which led to your reading these words, you will trace one primary motive. That motive is your basic desire for inner enlightenment. Even though you approach this study with great skepticism, even though your motive seems to be simply curiosity as to how the claims made as to the effectiveness of Tarot can be substantiated, your interest is primary founded upon that basic spiritual urge to seek Light.

This light-seeking impulse is the first requisite for success in the use of the Tarot. Only when such desire is aroused will the student have the patience to continue the practice work. The very fact that you are reading this instruction is ample proof that you are ready for it, because nothing ever happens by accident. It is a fundamental precept of occultism that when the student is ready his instruction will be forthcoming.

The aim of this instruction is to show you how to use the Tarot Keys for the purpose of evoking thought, and thus bringing to the surface of your consciousness, where you can see and understand them, those fundamental principles of occult science which lie hidden in the hearts of all mankind. All these principles are based upon a single truth, and knowledge of that truth is innate in every hu-

7

man being; but not until it has been found and brought into the light of consciousness is it available for use. Hence the portals of ancient temples bore the motto: "Know Thyself;" hence Jesus said, "Seek first into the Kingdom of God, which is within you."

Its rich symbolism and ingenious construction make the Tarot the best of all instruments for true occult education; that is, for drawing out the wisdom hidden within you. The practical instruction which you will be given will aid you greatly in the interpretation of these Keys. Into your hands will be put the clues which will lead to a deeper understanding of the Tarot and of the laws of life. You must follow these clues yourself. Only in this way will the Tarot bring out the knowledge that lies within you, and this knowledge is all that can possibly be of any importance to you.

To each prospector in this exhaustless mine of ageless wisdom, persevering study will reveal knowledge that another seeker might never discover. Hence, no matter how high may be his sources of information, no interpreter may declare, "This is the full and final explanation of the Tarot." There is no final explanation. No student can exhaust the possibilities of this extraordinary symbolic alphabet, any more than one person can exhaust the possibilities of any language. The most that any one can say is that there is a definite manner in which to approach the study of the cards, just as there are tunnels that lead to the heart of a gold mine. The function of this instruction is to provide a map, or plan of the mine. You who read must enter, and dig out the treasure for yourself.

Your first task must be to master the elements of the esoteric language of symbols in which the Tarot is written.

The first six months of your instruction will deal largely with this work. You must at all times pay particular attention, then, to instructions, and carry them out to the letter. Nothing will be given you to do that you cannot carry out with a clear conscience and without fear. If you do follow instructions, you will be most agreeably surprised at the change that six short months will make in your personality. You will find yourself developing the ability to concentrate; you will find yourself endowed with keener perceptions; with a greater comprehension of yourself and your experience of life.

A simple perusal of these words once a week as they are issued will be perfectly useless to you. You might far better save your time and energy. Unless you are willing to devote a certain period each day to this work, so that you can study your cards, it will be futile to expect results. "Out of nothing cometh nothing." In simple justice to yourself, prepare to enter into the spirit of Tarot practice.

Do these words sound discouraging? They are deliberately attempting to discourage the widely curious and the superficial. It has been wisely said, "A little knowledge is a dangerous thing." Do not delude yourself into believing that you have no time for this work. It is absurd to say that you have no time for the most important thing in your life, you own spiritual growth. You are probably proving this every day of your life by seek continually for greater enlightenment. You read books, you talk to people about it, attend meetings and lectures. Yet fifteen minutes a day devoted to Tarot study can give you more than hours of other activities. Your Tarot period is the one part of your day that you cannot <u>afford</u> to miss.

Your first practical exercise will be to memorize the following statements. Commit them to memory in the following manner: Read the entire passage from beginning to end, instead of trying to learn it piecemeal. Then try to say it over to yourself. Persist in this practice until you have it. Then write it down on paper. This exercise is the shortest way to memorize a passage. Take care to use it for this work, because it is a correct start for the organization of your conscious processes.

PATTERN ON THE TRESTLEBOARD

This is truth about the Self:

0. All the power that ever was or will be is here now.

1. I am a center of expression for the Primal Will-to-Good which eternally creates and sustains the universe.

2. <u>Through</u> me its unfailing Wisdom takes form in thought and word.

3. Filled with Understanding of its perfect law, I am guided moment by moment along the path of liberation.

4. From the exhaustless riches of its Limitless Substance, I draw all things needful, both spiritual and material.

5. I recognize the manifestation of the undeviating Justice in all the circumstances of my life.

6. In all things great and small I see the Beauty of the divine expression.

7. Living from that Will, supported by its unfailing Wisdom and understanding, mine is the Victorious Life.

8. I look forward with confidence to the perfect realization of the Eternal Splendor of the Limitless Light.

9. In thought and word and deed, I rest my life, from day to day, upon the sure Foundation of Eternal Being.

10. The Kingdom of Spirit is embodied in my flesh.

This Pattern should be used every morning upon arising, and every night before you go to sleep. Be sure to do this, even though it seems a foolish and unnecessary practice at present. Do not say it automatically, but make an attempt to think through the meaning of the words. Make this effort every time you recite it.

The next lesson will give you a greater insight into its inner meaning. The key to this will be in the numbering of the statements. We recommend that you study the Pattern on the Trestle Board in connection with the instruction next week. Secure a notebook, and write therein any interesting observations you may have. Be sure to put them in your notebook, no matter how trivial they may seem.

This notebook is IMPORTANT. It is your <u>occult diary</u>, and it will contain the record of your progress. This diary will be of tremendous importance to you in later practical work. To slight it is to defeat one of the main purposes of this instruction. Use it every time you study, and make an entry at that time, even if it is to record a failure to study at the time scheduled. You will be requested to send it to headquarters at intervals for comment and advice. Other than that, <u>do not show it to anyone</u>. Do not fail to heed these instructions to the letter.

If you have not already colored your Keys, you should begin to do so, in accordance with the instructions you received with them. If it should so happen that you secured your Keys before the coloring instructions were issued, send for a volume containing the history of Tarot, its chief attributions, a brief outline of the meanings of the Keys, complete coloring instructions and a set of colors, which may be had for 75 cents, directly from the School of Ageless Wisdom.

Colored keys are imperative for this work. The symbology connected with the color is highly important, besides the definite effect of the mental impression made by the action of the color impulses upon the cells of your brain. After the next lesson this instruction will proceed upon the assumption that you are using colored Keys.

Editors Note: You may purchase the black and white Tarot Keys referred to in this book and coloring instructions from the Builders of the Adytum by writing to them at 5105 N. Figueroa Street, Los Angeles, CA or by visiting the B.O.T.A. web site: www.bota.org

As of this printing, a complete set of B.O.T.A. Tarot Keys and coloring instructions can be downloaded free of charge at the following web site:
http://tarotinstitute.com/free/bota/index.html

THE SYMBOLISM OF NUMBERS

Number symbols represent truths at once simple and universal, truths immanent in all things and manifest in all phenomena. The science of number is at the foundation of practical occultism, as it is at the foundation of every department of human knowledge. Resolve to master thoroughly the elements of that science as presented in this lesson. Thus you will be taking an important step toward the understanding of cosmic law, which will eventually put you in harmony with the rhythms of the cosmic life-manifestation, make you the ruler of your personality, and free you from the limitations of your environment.

Let no fancied inaptitude or dislike for mathematics deters you from entering seriously into this study. You need not be quick at figures, nor do you require a natural bent for abstruse abstractions to undertake this work. You will be able to master the underlying principles in a comparatively short time. Practice will make you proficient in their various applications.

The numerals 0 to 9 represent successive stages in every cycle of evolution, whether on the grand scale of the cosmos, or on the smaller scale of personal unfoldment. The order in the numerical series reflects an order which prevails in creation. It is an ancient doctrine that the Master Builder has ordered all things by measure and number and weight. Throughout the structure of the universe the properties of number are manifested, whether in the revolution of planets around the sun, the whirling of electrons within the atom, in the crystallization of minerals, or in the arrangement of the parts of a living organism. Also, according to a famous relativist, a number is one of the few things in the universe which is not relative.

I shall attempt no exhaustive treatment of number symbolism in this elementary text. It would only bewilder you. What you need, for the present, is the outline of the meanings of the ten numeral signs. You can fill in the outline of number meanings as your proceed with your studies.

Some of the attributions may not be very clear at first. They may appear to be arbitrary and far-fetched. So do the meanings of all symbols when we first learn them. <u>Keep your purpose in view</u>. You are learning number symbols because they are part of the esoteric language which occultists have employed to transmit their knowledge from generation to generation. No satisfactory substitute for this language has been devised. By means of it an advanced occultist can communicate with a fellow-adept in spite of the barriers of ordinary language. With a few lines and figures he can express more meaning than he could speak into pages of words.

When you have fixed the fundamental ideas of this numerical system in your memory, you will soon learn that none are arbitrary. Then you will begin to see the connection between those ideas – which are printed in capitals at the beginning of each paragraph of attributions – and the other meanings which follow them. The discovery of the connections of these key ideas and the others are an important part of your mental training. You must make it for yourself.

MEANING OF THE NUMERAL SIGNS

0. NO-THING; absence of quantity, quality, or mass; freedom from every limitation, changelessness, the unknown, immeasurable, fathomless, infinite, eternal Source; the Rootless Root of existence; the sacred ellipse, representing the endless line of eternity; the Cosmic Egg; Super-consciousness.

1. BEGINNING; the first of the number series, because 0 stands for that which precedes all manifestation, and therefore is not properly included in the series; inception; initiative; selection; unity, singleness individuality; attention; one-pointedness; concentration; the definite, <u>or existent</u>, as contrasted with indefinable Source, which is <u>subsistent</u>; Self-consciousness.

2. DUPLICATION; repetition; reflection antithesis; opposition; polarity; continuation; succession; sequence; diffusion; separation; radiation; secondariness; subordination; dependence; Sub-consciousness.

3. MULTIPLICATION; increase; growth; augmentation; expansion; amplification; productiveness; fecundity; generation; the response of sub-consciousness to self-consciousness in the generation of mental images.

4. ORDER; system; regulation; management; supervision; control; authority; command; dominance; the classifying activity of self-consciousness, induced by the multiplication of mental images through the responding of the sub-consciousness to impression origi-

nating in self-consciousness. This classifying activity is <u>Reason</u>.

5. MEDIATION; (an idea suggested by the fact that 5 is the middle term in the series of signs from 1 to 9); adaptation; intervention; adjustment; accommodation; reconciliation; result of the classifying activities symbolized by 4. A sub-conscious elaboration of these classifications, and the formulation of deductions therefrom. Those deductions, projected into self-consciousness, are mental states termed <u>Intuitions</u>.

6. RECIPROCATION; interchange; correlation; response; coordination; cooperation; correspondence; harmony; concord; equilibration, symmetry, beauty.

7. EQUILIBRIUM; (the result of equilibration, the concrete application of the laws of symmetry and reciprocation); mastery; poise; rest; conquest; peace; safety; security; victory; art.

8. RHYTHM; periodicity; alternation; flux and reflux; pulsation; vibration; involution and evolution; education; culture; the response of sub-consciousness to everything symbolized by 7.

9. CONCLUSION; (literally, "closing together," and this implies the union of elements which are separate until the conclusion is reached. This has a bearing on certain meanings attached to the number 9 through the Tarot Key bearing this number); goal; end; completion; fulfillment; attainment; the final result of the process symbolized by the series of digits; perfection; procell symbolized by the series of digits; perfection; adeptship; the mystical "three times three" of the Free

Masons, and of other societies which preserve some fragments of the ancient mysteries.

The meaning of a number consisting of two or more digits may be ascertained by combining the ideas indicated by each symbol, beginning always with the digit in the right hand, or units place. Thus 10 combines the ideas of 0 and 1. Following 9, 10 shows that the finality symbolized by 9 refers only to a single cycle of manifestation. The completion of a cycle is always a return to the external Nothing, 0; but since this 0 is changeless in its inherent nature it is eternally a self-manifesting power, consequently a new cycle beings as soon as the previous cycle ends. Thus 10 symbolizes the eternal creativeness of the Life Power; the incessant whirling forth of the self-expression of the Primal Will; the ever-turning Wheel of Manifestation. (See the Tarot Key numbered 10). The number 10 is also a combination of the characteristic symbols of the masculine (1) and feminine (0) modes of life expression. Memorize the numbers and the Key words written in capitals.

<u>Set aside ten pages in your occult diary</u>. Head each page with one of the numeral signs and its key word. Then write in all that is written after each key word. This is important. To copy anything is to make it more surely yours than if you merely read it. Whenever you get an idea about the meaning of some number, make a note of it. Then see that it is entered in your notebook under the appropriate heading. You will be surprised at the amount of material that will seem to flow to you as if by magic upon the meaning of numbers. After a time you will hold these notes among the most valuable in your reference library.

Another good idea, in this connection, is to look up each word in the ten paragraphs in a dictionary. You will derive a great amount of insight from this exercise alone.

During your study period arrange your Tarot Keys in the following order:

			0			
1	2	3	4	5	6	7
8	9	10	11	12	13	14
15	16	17	18	19	20	21

Examine attentively, paying special attention to the numbers of the cards. Try to connect them with the pictures. In the numbers from 10 to 21, try to work out the meanings of the numbers from what you have been told about the various digits. Transcribe your findings into your notebook. Do this, no matter how trivial they may seem to you. You must make a beginning. These attempts of yours are seeds that will bear much good fruit later on.

In the above arrangement of the Tarot Keys you will note that the Zero card is placed above the others, to indicate that it precedes the whole series, and is not really in the sequence of numbers. For your information, though you may not be able to use it at first, the pictures in the top row refer to <u>powers</u> or <u>potencies</u> of consciousness; those in the middle row are symbols of <u>laws</u>, or <u>agencies</u>; those in the bottom row represent <u>conditions</u>, or effects. Thus 1 is the power which works through the agency of 8 to modify the conditions or effects represented by 15; 2 is the power which works through 9 to modify the conditions represented by 16; and so on through the entire series. Also notice that all Keys balance numerically through 11, which represents Justice, or Equilibrium. Thus 11 is ½ of the sum of any two numbers in the same position relative to that Key, as 1 and 21; 9 and 13; 16 and 6, etc.

In the next lesson we will proceed to the explanation of the separate pictures of the Tarot Keys.

THE LIFE POWER

The first thing to do before your read this lesson is to take your Tarot Key numbered 0, the Fool, and place it before you. Observe every detail closely, so that you can make mental reference to it as you read this lesson. Be orderly about it. Start with the Hebrew letter, which is Aleph, in the lower right hand corner, then the Title and the number. Work progressively from right to left, from the top of the picture to the bottom.

Key 0 represents the manner in which the Absolute presents itself, in a measure, to the wise. The Absolute is THAT about which nothing can be said, because IT entirely transcends finite comprehension. It is the Rootless Root of all being, the Causeless Cause of all that is, yet these names cannot in the least define IT. All speculations as to ITS nature are futile. But what is important to us is the way in which IT manifests ITSELF to our understanding.

Some of the names which have been given to this manifestation are as follows: the LIFE POWER; LIMITLESS LIGHT; L.V.X.; the ONE FORCE; the ONE THING; the PRIMAL WILL. Learn these names. They designate the force that you use in every thought, feeling, and action; the force which you will utilize in your Tarot practice. Your advancement will be measured strictly by your growing comprehension of the real meaning of these names.

The first symbol of the LIFE POWER is 0. Review what is listed under the numerical sign 0 in your lesson last week. There you will see the key word is NOTHING. The LIFE POWER is limitless. Therefore it is <u>nothing</u> we can define, <u>nothing</u> we can measure; <u>nothing</u> we can fathom, <u>nothing</u> that will ever come to an end, <u>nothing</u> which ever had a beginning.

0 looks like an egg, and an egg is something which contains the potencies of growth and development. As a living form is hatched from an egg, so is everything in the universe brought forth from the Cosmic Egg of the LIFE POWER. The LIFE POWER has within it <u>all</u> possibilities. All manifestation, every object, every force in the universe is an adaptation of the ONE LIFE POWER. Because its possibilities are truly limitless, it can be specialized in any particular form, or manifestation, of which the human mind can conceive. This is the reason why it is possible to achieve results by purely <u>mental</u> means.

Because the LIFE POWER is the force behind all manifestation, and consequently behind all growth, it is obviously Cultural Power. This is graphically portrayed by the attribution of the Hebrew letter Aleph to this Key. Aleph means "Ox." Oxen were the motive power in primitive agriculture. They were used to plow fields, to thresh grain, to carry burdens. Agriculture is the basic form of civilization, so the ox represents the power at work in all forms of human adaptation and modification of natural conditions. In this way the ox symbolizes creative energy, the vital principal in all forms of living creatures. This vital principle comes to us in physical form as the <u>energy of the sun</u>.

Consequently we see that the LIFE POWER is not an abstraction, far removed from our everyday life. We contact it everywhere, in every form. Our senses reveal it to us physically as light and heat from the sun, and scientific research makes known to everyone that sun energy is the basis of our physical existence.

Just as sunlight is a form of electro-magnetic vibration, measurable with physical instruments, so is every other part of the universe, physical or super physical, composed also of electro-magnetic vibrations which quickly pass beyond the range of any man-made instrument. But there is an instrument, not made by man, which <u>can</u> utilize and adapt these higher vibrations, this <u>radiant mental energy</u>, in a manner truly wonderful. That instrument is the human personality, and you are its possessor. Its function is to give free expression to the LIFE POWER (recall statements 0, 1 and 2 of the Pattern on the Trestle Board.)

One of the most important forms taken by this energy, and the first one you should learn to use, is AIR. You must learn to control actual <u>atmospheric air</u>, or, in other words, learn to breathe properly. We do not recommend here that you indulge in any of the various breathing exercises recommended by many teachers of occult development. They have no place in your instruction at this time, since they only too often prove dangerous to students who do not fully realize what they are attempting. It is important just to learn to breathe deeply, filling the lungs with air and providing the blood stream with oxygen it requires. Practice this consistently and you will soon breathe properly automatically.

The important of breath is shown in the symbolism of The Fool. Aleph is the special sign of Air in Hebrew esoteric philosophy. The noun "Fool" is derived from the Latin word "follies" meaning "a bag of wind." Follis also means "bellows" which is an instrument for the utilization of air. The yellow tint in the background is also symbolical of air. Add to this the fact that, in every civilized language, wise men use the words which ordinarily mean <u>air</u>, <u>wind</u>, or <u>breath</u> to designate <u>life</u>, or <u>conscious energy</u>, and you can readily fathom the significance attached to air by occultists, and realize the importance of learning to use it properly.

The Tarot title for the LIFE POWER is highly ingenious. It tells us all that we need to know, at the same time throwing the idly curious or the superficial completely off the track. One key to the true significance of the title "THE FOOL" is the say, "The Wisdom of God is foolishness with men." Thus it is that those men, found in every generation who gain an unusual knowledge of the LIFE POWER are usually called madmen or <u>fools</u> by their less enlightened brethren.

So this title hints at a state of consciousness which has even been termed pathological by some materialistic psychologists, simply because its results were unfamiliar to them and they were totally incapable of understanding it. This state of consciousness is termed, by those who can comprehend its significance, as "Super-consciousness" or "Cosmic Consciousness." To attain such a state of consciousness is to comprehend the universe in its entirety, and to gain complete self-realization. The attainment of

Super-consciousness may well be given as the ultimate object of your Tarot study. You must not understand, by that, that some method of instruction or practice outside yourself is going to bring you Super-consciousness in some miraculous manner. Nothing could be farther from the truth. To study will help you gradually to organize the powers of your personality so that you will be able to express Super-consciousness through it.

The only way that we can conceive of the Absolute is in terms of our own experience. We always tend to invest IT with human form, from the highest ideas of a creator to the grossest anthropomorphism. This is what is symbolized by the Fool himself. Behind this personal seeming, however, the sages discern something higher – typified in this picture as the white Sun – an Impersonal Power, manifesting as the Limitless Energy radiated to the planets of innumerable world-systems by their suns. In manifestation that Energy, symbolized also by the fair hair of the traveler, is temporarily limited by living organisms, of these the vegetable kingdom, represented by the green wreath, is the primary class from which, in the order of evolution, spring animal organisms typified by the red feather.

The LIFE POWER is forever young, forever in the morning of its power, forever on the verge of the abyss of manifestation. It always faces unknown possibilities of self-expression transcending any height which it might previously have reached. Hence the Fool faces west (the direction of the unknown) toward a peak at which he gazes, above and beyond his present station. It is that which was, is, and shall be, and this is indicated by the Hebrew letters IHVH (Yod-Heh-Vau-Heh) at the collar of his undergarment, which have that meaning. This inner robe is the dazzling white light of Perfect Wisdom. It is concealed by the black coat of ignorance, lined with the red of passion and material force. This outer garment is embroidered with a floral decoration, but the unit of design is a solar orb containing eight red spokes, and symbolizing the initial whirling motion that brings the universe into manifestation. This outer garment is held on by a girdle consisting of twelve units, seven of which are showing. This girdle symbolizes Time, and it is only when man is freed from the limitation of time that he is able to overcome ignorance and passion. Other details of this picture are outlined in the booklet you received with your Tarot Keys. Study them in connection with this Key.

During your practice period this week read this lesson once each day. Pay particular attention to anything that may seem obscure to you, and endeavor to think it through. Give complete attention to everything stated, and set down in your notebook anything that may occur to you in connection with this lesson.

The most important part of your work, however, will be the study of the Key itself. Devote at least five minutes to that before commencing to read the lesson. It is far more important to imprint the details of the Key upon your brain cells than it is to gain an intellectual grasp of their significance. The reason for this will develop as you continue with the instruction. There is only one way to make such an impression, and that is to look at the Key and observe its details carefully. It is particularly important to place in your notebook any thoughts which may occur to you during your study of the card itself. Do not neglect any of these instructions.

Before you look at your Key, place yourself comfortably in a chair, preferably one with a straight back. Sit with both feet squarely on the floor, and take several deep breaths, exhaling slowly. Try to see that there is <u>fresh</u> air in the room, because breath of air that is stale is but little better than no breath at all. Do not shift about constantly nor cross your knees. Sit naturally and restfully. It is entirely unnecessary to hold yourself rigidly, either physically or mentally; yet you should not adopt a posture of complete relaxation. Have observed these preliminaries you will be able to devote your attention to your Tarot Key without giving your body any further thought.

There is one other exercise with the Fool that is earnestly recommended to you. This practice is to be used every day, not for this week only. Just after reciting your Pattern on the Trestle Board each morning look at the 'The Fool' for a few minutes. Do the same thing before reciting it at night. You will find this practice very beneficial, because The Fool sums up all of the meanings of the Pattern. In this way you will impress upon your consciousness, with doubled strength, the Truth about the Self.

SELF-CONSCIOUSNESS

Begin this lesson in the same manner that you did the last, by considering in detail Key number 1, the MAGICIAN.

Consideration of the number, 1, will tell you that this Key must have something to do with beginning or inception. This is true, because it represents the initiation of the creative process on all planes of Nature. The creative process in the individual is initiated by the phase of consciousness which we shall term self-consciousness, or the OBJECTIVE MIND. Self is the distinctly human aspect of mental activity. It is the waking mind, which you are using to read these pages.

Self-consciousness initiates the creative process by formulating premises, or seed ideas. These subconsciousness accepts as suggestions, elaborates by the process of deduction, and carries out in physiological function and organization. These two sentences outline a most important process. You use it continually without knowing that you do, because it is the basis of your intellectual knowledge as well as the state of your physical health. All of your physical and mental states are the results of your mental imagery; and you have the clue to success in occult practice when you thoroughly understand what is implied by the statement that ANY MEN-

TAL IMAGE TENDS TO MATERIALIZE ITSELF AS AN ACTUAL CONDITION OR EVENT.

Geometrically the number 1 is a point, particularly a central point. In the Pattern on the Trestle Board the statement attributed to the number 1 is, "I am a <u>center of expression</u> for the Primal Will to good which eternally creates and sustains the universe." The beginning of the creative process is the collection of the LIFE POWER at a center, and Its expression through that center. The sun of our solar system is such a center. It transmits the LIFE POWER in a form in which It can be utilized.

The idea is shown in two ways by the Hebrew letter Beth. Ancient forms of this character represented an arrow head, which clearly represents a point. The letter name means "house", which is a definite location used as an abode. In the sense used here it refers to whatever form may be used as a dwelling place for Spirit, and the form particularly referred to in this lesson is the <u>human personality</u>. The personality is a center through which the Spirit, or Real Self of man, expresses Itself. Do not be abstract about this. Think of <u>your</u> personality as a <u>center of expression</u> of your Inner Self. Try to realize what Jesus meant when He said, "The Father Who dwelleth within me, He doeth the works."

The title of this Key, THE MAGICIAN, definitely identifies the picture with Hermes, or Mercury, who presided over Magic. You will remember that Mercury was the messenger of the gods and in this capacity served to <u>transmit</u>, or <u>express</u>, their wisdom. This identification with Hermes is also connected with two meanings of number 1 as privacy or concealment, and thus occult knowledge. <u>Magic</u> is the art of <u>transformation</u>, and it is closely related to the Hermetic art alchemy. Self-consciousness is the transformer. It and it alone, is able to set in motion the forces which bring about change, variation, etc. The fundamental magical practice is CONCENTRATION, or one-pointed attention to some selected area of one's environment.

The practice of concentration enables one to perceive the inner nature of the object of his attention, thus leading to the discovery of the natural principles which, when applied, enable us to change conditions. The higher phases of this are those which have to do with the underlying principles of human existence. Thus the reason you are using the Tarot Keys as objects of concentration is that they represent the basic modes of human consciousness.

Learn the following definition: CONCENTRATION IS THE COLLECTION AT A CENTER, OR FOCUS, OF UNITS OF FORCE. These units are always units of the LIFE POWER, because every unit in the universe, regardless of the form it takes, is made of the ONE FORCE. Thus you will understand that you do not concentrate attention. Attention is the means which enables you to concentrate units of mental energy. The result is that you intensify this energy so that you can direct it usefully. When you intensify the rays of the sun through a convex lens, they will burn your hand if you direct them upon it, but if you place your hand in the sunlight passing through a pane of window glass, the resulting sensation is merely a slight feeling of warmth. Never forget that you are directing a real force when you practice concentration.

Note the posture of the Magician in Key 1. With his right hand he draws power from above. With his left he makes the gesture of concentration. He is directing his power to a plane below that of his own existence for a specific reason. This picture shows clearly the magical process involved in an understanding of the correct use of the practice of concentration. The plane below the Magician is shown as a garden, which typifies sub-consciousness. When you concentrate you always seek to impress some definite image upon sub-consciousness, thus accomplishing some definite modification of the sub-conscious field of activity. You will understand this more completely next week, when we shall consider some of the powers of sub-consciousness.

The table represents the field of attention, which is the Magician's workbench. Upon it are the implements which he uses. There are Will (wand), Imagination (cup), Action (sword), and Form (pentacle). All transformations are dependent upon the ability of the objective mind to produce variations of these four elements.

The roses in the garden are red, to symbolize active desire which is the power that spurs us to accomplishment. Five are shown, because all desires spring from some kind of sensation. Every rose represents the number 5 (see lesson 2 on numbers) since that number governs the development of the petals. 5 is the number of Man and of his power to control the forces of Nature. It is the great magical number.

The white lilies represent abstract perceptions of truth, or principles and laws. They also represent the number 6 because that number governs the development of their flowers. 6 represents, symbolically, universal forces, such as are familiar upon this plane as light, heat, electricity and chemical forces.

34

The garments of the Magician show that the outer aspect of the LIFE POWER utilized in the practice of concentration is the active desire nature, while the inner reality is the white brilliance of the Primal Will. The serpent girdle is a symbol of eternity, and of the limitation of form imposed upon the One Force in all practice of concentration.

The black hair of the Magician symbolizes inertia, ignorance, and darkness, which is limited by the white band of enlightenment. The horizontal figure eight above his head represents dominion, strength and control. It is the mathematical symbol of infinity, that is, of the limitless Life Power. It like-wise represents the law that opposite effects are produced by identical causes. The same law that makes iron sink is used by ship builders in order to float iron ships; the law that makes a kite fall to the ground is utilized in aviation; the laws that result in disease, misery and failure are those which intelligent adaptation employs in order to manifest health, happiness and success.

The arbor of roses is connected with the meanings of the letter Beth, since an arbor is the simplest kind of shelter, or house. The red roses suggest that the power which the Magician draws from above is modified by desire. This is true of all self-conscious activity. Every moment of our waking consciousness is motivated and conditioned by some type of desire.

The two points of the Magician's rod, as well as the red roses at the top and bottom of the picture symbolize one of the most important of the Hermetic axioms, THAT WHICH IS ABOVE IS AS THAT WHICH IS BELOW.

Be sure to learn this axiom. It is a key to the understanding of many occult secrets.

Astrologically the planet Mercury is attributed to this Key. Mercury is said to rule the intellect and all of the functions of the objective mind. Thus it represents the mental power exercised in concentration, mathematics, constructive planning, all the sciences and all observations. Alchemical mercury is the metal attributed to the Magician, and this metal was reputed to hold a key position in the transmutation of base metals into gold. Try to penetrate the meaning of this symbolical attribution. Write in your notebook what you believe its meaning to be.

The yellow background refers to the intellect, to Air, and to the radiant mental energy that comes to us as sunlight. This color represents the same ideas wherever it is used in the Tarot.

Read this lesson once daily during your practice period this week. Before doing so be sure to look at the Tarot Key for five minutes. There is enough material in this lesson for a great deal of careful study. Do not slight it because you think you understand it thoroughly after one or two readings. Such will not be the case, as you will readily find out by following up some of the lines of thought indicated here. It is important that you give the statements made in this lesson your most careful attention, because they tell you how to begin successful practical work, and unless you understand the beginning, it is quite useless to attempt to understand any part working thereof.

You may begin your practice of concentration this week by focusing your attention upon some particular detail of the picture. Examine it attentively, and try to think of everything you can in connection with it. Determine its shape, color, and any other physical sensation you connect with it. Compare it with similar objects and contrast it with unlike objects. Determine its relationship to other parts of the picture or to any of the other Tarot Keys. Develop the meaning of the symbol as given in this lesson and in your Tarot booklet. Write down any interesting ideas which may come to you in this connection. Use different part of the key each day.

This exercise is optional. Do it or not as you desire. If you do it you will receive a great deal of benefit from the practice. It is the aim of this instruction to supply the necessary elementary work in Tarot, and at the same time to provide practical instruction of a more advanced type for those who are ready to avail themselves of it.

It is never necessary to strain in order to concentrate; instead of screwing up your face and clenching your fists as though you expected the practice to require the use of your physical strength, simply forget about your body and calmly direct your attention to the object upon which you desire to concentrate. The main thing is not to allow your attention to waver. Check such tendency by bringing your attention back as soon as you catch yourself thinking about anything irrelevant to your subject. Do not become discouraged if you will find this difficult. You would have more cause for surprise if you did not find it so.

SUB-CONSCIOUSNESS

Consider the symbolism of Key 2, the High Priestess, before you read this lesson.

Among the meanings of the number 2, as given to you on in lesson 2, is SUBORDINATION. This word gives you the clue to the relationship existing between sub-consciousness, represented Key 2, and self-consciousness, represented by the Magician. The figure in Key 1 is engaged in controlling the powers of sub-consciousness, and these powers are always amenable to his suggestive influence. It is because of this fact that you are able to use these Keys to bring into vigorous manifestation the latent forces of your inner life. The principle involved here may be formulated as follows: SUB-CONSIOUSNESS IS PERFECTLY AMENABLE TO CONTROL BY SUGGESTION.

This psychological law makes obvious the fact that the important thing is to be careful about the kind of suggestions which you formulate in your self-conscious mind, since that is the main source of the suggestions received by sub-consciousness. This phase of consciousness, you will recall, is represented by the garden in Key 1. The fertile soil of this garden <u>will grow any seed planted in it by the Magician</u>. Thus if you plant careless observations and incorrect reasoning, which are symbolic tares or weeds, sub-consciousness will develop theses seeds of error a thousand fold, with all sorts of uncomfortable conse-quences. On the other hand if you learn to concentrate, to make your mental imagery clear and definite, if you make accurate observations from which you draw correct infe-rences, the seeds that will be thus planted in sub-consciousness will be reflected in processes that lead to the renewal, revivification, and regeneration of your per-sonality.

The ability of sub-consciousness to develop seed ideas in this manner can be formulated thus: SUB-CONSCIOUSNESS IS POSSESSED OF PERFECT POWERS OF DEDUCTIVE REASONING. If you are not certain of the difference between deductive and inductive reasoning, be sure to consult a good dictionary before you proceed further. Always, when you study, have a dictio-nary at hand, for you will need it frequently in the course of this instruction. You will find this practice alone to be of immeasurable benefit to you in the orderly organization of your mental processes.

Geometrically the number 2 is the <u>line</u>, which is the extension of the <u>point</u> (number 1). This suggests the sub-conscious power just mentioned of developing the conse-quences of conscious thought and observation. You will not fail to note that the extension of the central point of a circle into a diameter (an extension in two directions) di-vides the circle into <u>two</u> parts, each the exact <u>duplicate</u> of the other. In this faculty of sub-conscious, duplications can be perceived the basic function of sub-consciousness – MEMORY. This brings us to the third psychological principle, SUB-CONSCIOUSNESS KEEPS A PERFECT RECORD OF ALL EXPERIENCE, AND THEREFORE HAS PERFECT MEMORY. Not only does it retain all of the experience of the individual, but contains also a summary of the Race Experience, which is the source of the greater part of our intuitions and scientific discoveries.

Much of the symbolism in the High Priestess is directly connected with Memory. Her scroll contains the complete record of experience, but two things are requisite if you are to read it. First you must practice concentration. By careful observation and vivid awareness of what goes on around you, you focus your mental camera, and the resulting images are sharp and clear. Secondly you must understand and apply the law of recall. Let us examine these laws in the terms of the symbolism of the Key.

The pillars represent two of the laws by their form and color, and another law by their position. You can easily recall ideas or things that are LIKE each other; ideas or things in sharp CONTRAST to each other; ideas or things NEAR each other in space or time. Here are three rules in practical mnemonics. If you use these identification tags consciously when you file your experiences you can make a mental index that will give you the ability to recall any phase of your experience at will. Link the think you want to recollect with something like it. Contrast it with something decidedly different. Notice what things are near it in time and space.

Now examine the symbols on the veil behind the High Priestess. The members of the pattern are repetitions of the two symbols used (pomegranates and palm leaves which symbolize opposite forces and consequently the law of contrast). The fourth law of recall is frequency. In the first lesson of this instruction you had the opportunity to put this law into practice when you learned the Pattern of the Trestle Board. Along with frequency goes recency,

41

since we tend to recall recent experiences more readily than others.

All of these laws of memory are various processes of association. The Hebrew Letter assigned to Key 2 is Gimel. It means camel. The camel is called the "ship of the desert" because it is used to connect distant points for purposes of commerce and transportation. In this meaning can be read the fourth great power of sub-consciousness, which can be stated thus: SUB-CONSCIOUSNESS HAS PERFECT CONNECTION WITH ALL POINTS IN SPACE. This law is the basis of the phenomenon of mental telepathy. It is also the law that puts you into touch with your true Teacher when you have developed to the point where you are ready for higher instruction.

In this connection it will be well to dwell for a moment upon a very important fact. If you understand this fact you will have a clue to the tremendous powers of consciousness which are within your reach provided you make the necessary effort that will bring you to the knowledge of the principles which underlie them. Your personal sub-consciousness contains the record of your personal experience. But your personal sub-consciousness is comparable to a small bay in an inconceivably vast ocean. The ocean is the UNIVERSAL SUB-CONSCIOUSNESS. Hence, when you have learned how, you can gain access to the records of all of the experience of the universe through tapping the cosmic or universal MEMORY. This is the ability to read the "Akashic Records", which is the name occultists give to the Universal Memory. If you are versed in the occult teachings with regard to these records you will find many clues in Key 2 that will lead you to the knowledge of the true nature of Akasha.

There is one law which operates to enable such universal association and intercommunication. That law is closely bound up with all of the meanings of the number 2 and is graphically symbolized by the robe of the High Priestess. The robe represents Water, which is in turn a symbol of ROOT MATTER, or Prakriti as the Hindus call it. Its wavy form represents VIBRATION. This is one of the most important words in all occultism. We live in a vibratory universe, and it is vibratory activity in the ROOT MATTER that brings us into touch with other points in the universe, just as such vibration brings us into touch with the source of life in our solar system, the Sun.

The ROOT MATTER is identical with SUB-CONSCIOUSNESS, of which water is also a symbol. Water was the first mirror, and because mirroring is duplication, or reflection it is closely related to all of the meanings of number 2. It is conscious energy of the ONE FORCE, acting upon itself in its subconscious aspect of ROOT MATTER that brings into being all physical structures, INCLUDING THE CELLS OF YOUR BODY.

The function of every cell is the result of the LIFE POWER flowing through that cell. From this it follows that SUBCONSCIOUSNESS KNOWS ALL ABOUT, AND CONTROLS EVERY BODILY ACTIVITY. This is the secret of all mental healing. It explains why thoughts have such an important bearing upon health. Since subconsciousness is perfectly amenable to control by suggestion, it transforms your conscious ideas about the state of your health into actual physical conditions.

Be sure that you understand what has been said in this lesson about the powers of sub-consciousness. Copy the definitions, which are written in capital letters, into your notebook and commit them to memory. Watch your daily experience closely and will soon be able to detect the operation of these principles in your own life. As you become increasingly familiar with them and the way the work you will put them more and more into conscious operation, with the result that you will gain ever greater control over the forces of your personality. Persistent practice in directing your personal forces involves the eventual attainment of extraordinary control over physical forces and conditions by <u>purely mental means</u>.

The predominant color of Key 2 is blue, which is that attributed to the letter Gimel. This color is always associated in occultism with Water and Sub-consciousness.

The veil behind the High Priestess is a symbol of virginity. It also symbolizes the associative powers of sub-consciousness. Pomegranates and palm leaves are embroidered upon it which are respectively feminine and masculine symbols. Note, however, that the pomegranates are red, color of Mars, which is a masculine color, while the palms are green, representing the feminine Venus vibration. This is only one of the many places in Key 2 which represents graphically the UNION OF OPPOSITE FORCES. The veil itself, because it joins the two pillars, is such a symbol.

The pillars, which are alike in form but opposite in color, symbolize all pairs of opposites, such as light and darkness, attraction and repulsion, affirmation and negation, active and passive, manifest and unmanifest. In each of the foregoing pairs the first is represented by the white pillar and the other by the black one. The letters upon them are Yod on the white and Beth on the black. These have Masonic significance.

The lotus buds at the top of the pillars refer to the subconscious activity which is the cause of all growth and development in organic life. They are buds, because this Key represents the <u>potencies</u> or <u>possibilities</u> of subconsciousness apart from their actual manifestation in response to conscious stimulation.

The cubic stone upon which the High Priestess sits is important in symbolism. Its meanings are too extended to go into here at length. STONE is an esoteric word meaning union, life, and wisdom. It is a symbol of the material world, and its shape suggests Salt, because salt always crystallizes in cubes, and Salt is an age-old symbol of Sub-consciousness and Matter.

The robe symbolizes <u>flowing</u> and <u>fluidity</u> and represents the ever changing forms of life expression. This robe is the source of all of the streams in Tarot.

The crown is of silver, and represents by its form the waxing and waning lunar crescents with the full moon between. These suggest periodicity and alternation, as well as the reflecting and reproductive power of subconsciousness. The Moon actually polarizes sunlight, so here is another reference to the polarity symbolized by the number 2.

The cross on her breast is white to represent Light. It symbolizes the union of the four elements represented by the four implements upon the table of the magician.

The scroll represents memory, history, and the record of experience. The word TORA signifies LAW, and is a rearrangement of the letters of the word ROTA, the Latin for "Wheel". This is the reference to the Law of Cycles, or Rotation, which will be more extensively dealt with later on. This Law of Cycles is closely connected with the Law of Spiral Activity, represented by the rolled-up scroll. Both these laws are aspects of the great Law of Rhythm.

Contemplate Key 2 for five minutes each day before reading this lesson. When you have studied the lesson place Keys 1 and 2 side by side. See how many contrasts you can find in the two pictures. Write those which you notice into your notebook. This practice is valuable both to improve your powers of observation and to establish in your consciousness the reciprocal relationship existing between these two Keys.

CREATIVE IMAGINATION

This week look at The Empress for five minutes before reading this lesson.

In Lesson 2 the key word attributed to the number 3 is MULTIPLICATION. The dictionary definition for mul-tiply is, "to cause to increase in number, to make more by natural generation." Multiplication is the act or operation of increasing by multiplying.

CREATIVE IMAGINATION is the way the principle of multiplication manifests itself in your consciousness. The secret of the process is given under the definitions of number 3 where it says "the response of Sub-consciousness to Self-consciousness in the generation of mental images." Just as 3 is produced by the combination of 1 and 2 so also is the Empress a symbolic combination of the ideas represented by the Magician and the High Priestess. Here is shown the activity which is the logical result of their harmonious union.

The High Priestess is a virgin. She symbolizes the po-tencies and possibilities of sub-consciousness rather than the actual exercise and unfoldment of those powers. For it is only when subconscious power are set in motion by the objective mind, the Magician, that their highest manifestation is possible.

Read the last sentence again. It is a brief and accurate statement of the reason why human beings are truly "lords of creation"; Man is the only being on earth that has an adequate organ for expressing self-consciousness. Consequently he is the only one who can <u>deliberately</u> modify his sub-consciousness to any appreciable extent. Man has, as his <u>birthright</u>, the ability to use intelligently the principles and forces which have worked for millions upon millions of years in transforming living organisms from simple, one-celled bodies to the human level of complexity. As man progresses in this development he begins to learn consciously to direct the transformation of his own organism, modifying it little by little until it is capable of receiving and utilizing forms of energy which will make him master of his environment and absolute lord of his destiny. At the present time you are at the beginning of this stage of conscious modification of you bodily organisms, for that is what these studies will help you to do. Such modification is brought about through the principles laid down in the lesson last week which you copied into your notebook. Review them before you proceed.

Imagination is the working out into active manifestation of the patterns impressed upon Sub-consciousness by self-consciousness. The progeny of the Empress are the concrete ideas that bring <u>illumination</u> and <u>understanding</u>. Imagination, because it is a subconscious process, is always deductive. It always reasons from the general to the particular. Failure to recognize this law frequently causes many of those who attempt to attain results by mental means to fall short of their goal. It is useless to affirm an absolute principle. To say over and over again, "All is Good" is just a vain repetition. <u>A statement of truth does not work unless it be linked to a specific image of some manifestation of the principle involved</u>. The image must be definite and <u>concrete</u>. It must prepare mind and body for action.

On this account the ten affirmations that constitute the Pattern on the Trestle Board lead by suggestion to specific changes in personal consciousness. True affirmations must be <u>patterns</u>. To say "All is Beauty" may be true, but it will not make your world a whit more beautiful. But to say "In all things, great and small, <u>I see</u> the Beauty of the Divine Expression," and to follow up this initial statement with specific images of beauty is to bring about a <u>transformation</u> of personal consciousness which will eventually modify for the better all things in <u>your</u> world.

The Hebrew letter DALETH (pronounced daw-layth) means "Door" in Hebrew. As applied to Key 3, it is the point of passage from the Within, or subjective world, to the Without, or objective world. This is precisely the function of imagination. We do not see sub-consciousness at work. All that we perceive is the end results, which present themselves to us as concrete mental images. Consequently, THE POINT WHERE THE WORKING POWER OF SUBCONSCIOUSNESS MAY BE CONTROLLED IS THE POINT WHERE THOUGHTS TAKE FORM AS DEFINITE MENTAL IMAGES. Ponder this statement. It tells you again why it is so important for you to discriminate as to the mental images to which you devote your attention. When you exercise your power of choice in this respect you take the most important step towards the complete control of your inner powers.

Daleth signifies the <u>door of life</u>. The Book of Tokens says, "Now, as Daleth, I present myself as the Portal, through which Life Eternal and Unbounded entereth the realm of temporal and limited creation. That great Door is… the fruitful Mother of all living." Again the same book states "She is the Thought, which spinneth the plan of existence, that web of manifestation which entangleth the minds of fools, and giveth understanding to the wise who know the secret of its mystery."

This is a plain indication that the Empress is Mother Nature. Astrologically she is Venus, goddess of Nature. The web of manifestation which entangles the minds of fools is illusion. The wise see through appearances and to them Nature unveils herself. The veil that conceals truth is the veil of human ignorance, and that veil can be removed by proper selection of mental imagery. The creative force is always at work in nature, but the application of that force is up to the individual man, since sub-consciousness has no power of discrimination.

The color of Key 3 is green, which is also the predominant color in nature. Note that green is produced by the combination of blue and yellow, which are the colors attributed respectively to the High Priestess and the Magician.

The Empress is a matronly figure, and traditional interpretations tell us that she is pregnant. She is therefore in direct contrast to the virginal High Priestess. This is in direct harmony with the fact that creative imagination is the direct result of the impregnation of the subconscious mind by self-consciousness.

Her hair is yellow like that of the Fool, symbolizing radiant energy. It is bound by a wreath of myrtle, a plant sacred to Venus. Myrtle is an evergreen shrub, and is thus a symbol of immortality.

On her head is a crown of twelve golden six-pointed stars. This connects her with the woman in Revelation, who was clothed with the sun and crowned with twelve stars, with the moon under her feet. Older symbolic representations identify her with the Queen of Heaven. Six-pointed stars represent universal forces; hence the symbolism of the crown is the twelve modes of cosmic activity which are associated with the twelve signs of the zodiac. One idea conveyed here is that sub-consciousness is not only affected by objective mind, but receives also an influx of power from the super-conscious, or celestial, level of the Life Power's activity.

Her green robe is bound by a golden girdle, above which there is shown a red triangle. The triangle, by its shape, is a Greek letter Delta, which corresponds to Daleth. It is red to show the influence of the universal fiery energy in the activities of sub-consciousness.

Her sceptre is surmounted with a globe bearing a cross. This is a symbol of dominion. Older symbolism is that the globe and cross form a union of masculine (cross) and feminine (globe) or positive and negative modes of the activity of the Life of Power on all planes of nature.

The shield is of copper, the metal sacred to Venus. The dove on its face, also sacred to Venus, is a symbol of the Holy Spirit in Christian symbology. The significance of this symbol in this connection is profound.

Beneath the feet of the Empress is a crescent moon. It represents the fact that all of the activities of sub-consciousness which have to do with growth, development, reproduction, and imagination are based upon rhythm.

The stone seat is richly ornamented, in contrast to the severe cube upon which the High Priestess is sitting. This shows the result of the operation of self-consciousness upon sub-consciousness, which results in modifications and adaptations of nature. That is why Venus is the goddess of art and beauty.

The ripened wheat in the foreground represents the completion of a cycle of growth, and carries with it the same idea of multiplication that is indicated by the number three.

The stream and pool in the background correspond to the stream of consciousness which has its source in the robe of the High Priestess. The symbol of water falling into a pool is also a subtle intimation of the male and female modes of the cosmic energy. The stream is modified and directed by the self-conscious activities represented by the Magician, and the pool represents the accumulation of these self-conscious influences in sub-consciousness. The stream waters the garden and makes it fertile.

The cypress trees in the background, the rosebush and the necklace of pearls are all Venusian symbols. The roses represent the seven astrological planets.

You will find that regular use of the Empress will enrich your faculty of creative imagination and stimulate your inventiveness. It will give you power to make new combinations of ideas, and to develop old ideas into something better. There is no picture in the entire series which is more needed in these days. We live in an age when cheap printing and motion pictures, combined with the cut-and-dried life of our cities, are endangering our imaginative power. We take our imagination at second-hand from the screen and the printed page. In direct consequence of this consulting psychologists are continually called upon to help in the solution of personal problems which have arisen simply because people do not realize the tremendous power of imagination. Our prisons are full simply because men and women are unable to imagine the consequences of their own acts. People fail in business and in other activities for the same reason.

This Key will help you to use Imagination positively and constructively. Through your eyes it tells your subconscious mind what powers it has and how they should be exercised. Possibly you may not grasp the inner meanings of the symbols at first. But <u>YOUR SUB-CONSCIOUSNESS WILL</u>, for this picture, like the other Tarot Keys, is in <u>YOUR SUBCONSCIOUS MIND'S OWN LANGUAGE</u>. Pictorial symbolism is the language of dream, of revery, of imagination. <u>It is not an intellectual affair, although intellect may analyze it</u>. It goes far deeper. Use Key 3 whenever you find yourself apparently sterile of ideas, and it will help to bring ideas to you in abundance.

REASON

This week use Key 4, The Emperor, as the basis of your five minute meditation before taking up the lesson.

The key word of the number 4 is ORDER, and closely allied meanings are system, regulation, management, supervision; also the classifying activity of self-consciousness, <u>induced by the multiplication of mental images</u> through the response of sub-consciousness to impressions <u>originating</u> in self-consciousness. This classifying activity is REASON.

A moment's consideration will make obvious the fact that mental imagery is useful to use chiefly after it has been <u>systematized</u>, or put in <u>order</u>. Then it becomes useful to us in our daily lives in the <u>regulation</u>, <u>supervision</u> and <u>management</u> of our affairs. When mental imagery is not so systematized we are creatures of our emotions and desires; impractical dreamers, unable to meet adequately the problems which life presents to us. We are <u>reasonable</u> men and women only when we are able to face life's experiences <u>squarely</u>.

The Emperor is an executive. Emperor means "he who sets in order" which is the chief function of an administrative officer. Thus the title is closely bound up with the meanings of the number 4. That which he administers is the progeny of the Empress. She is his consort, subject to her husband, <u>and her motherhood depends upon him</u>. On the other hand his sovereignty depends upon her mother-hood. Unless the universal subconscious activities bring forth the universe, the universal self-consciousness has nothing to govern. It is because she brings forth that he has something to rule.

This is true also in man, who is called in occult termi-nology the Microcosm, or little universe. The <u>activity</u> of imagination is subconscious response to impulses origi-nating in the acts of attention and observation carried out by the objective mind (the Magician). But the Magician (who appears later as the Emperor) would have nothing to control or transform if sub-consciousness did not send up from its depths a <u>stream of images</u> to be classified and ar-ranged by the Emperor. Thus, in Key 4, we find the Em-peror seated upon a height <u>overlooking</u> a stream <u>in his dominion</u> which originates in the robe of the High Pries-tess and <u>flows through</u> the garden of the Empress.

Geometrically the number 4 symbolizes a square which is a symbol of the physical plane and of concrete things in general. Concrete mental images in definite logi-cal order – "precept upon precept, line upon line" – are the basis of reason and common sense. The number 4 is also closely connected with the idea of <u>measurement,</u> and it is by means of reason that we are able to take the measure of our experience in order to interpret it correctly. Without such right measurement of experience we continue to mis-take the illusory for the real, and thus manifest all sorts of conditions which bring poverty, misery and disease.

The Hebrew letter Heh (pronounced hay) means win-dow. A window admits light (knowledge) and air (The Life Breath, Spirit) into the House (Beth) of the personali-ty. It also permits outlook, survey, supervision, etc. The function of SIGHT is attributed the Heh, which is closely allied to the idea of a window. It is also allied closely to reason. When our reasoning faculty is turn upon a subject so that we understand it we automatically say, "I see." We are strikingly reminded of the importance of sight in this connection in the 29th chapter of Proverbs where it is stated "Where there is no vision, the people perish."

The letter Heh is used, in the Hebrew language, exactly as is the English definite article "the". Reason is a <u>defining</u> faculty. This shows us, first of all, that it is a phase of self-conscious activity because to define anything is to <u>name</u> it, and self-consciousness is always associated in occultism with Adam, the namer. There is a curious colloquial expression one often hears which is usually used thoughtlessly in connection with something unknown or queer. The expression is "Name it, and it's yours." Whatever the origin of the statement, it is an actual truth when we understand the true meaning of naming anything. It will pay you to meditate upon this idea.

Definition limits, sets boundaries, specializes, particularizes and enters into details. The qualities thus indicated are precisely those which enter into the making of a constitution for any social organization from an entire nation on down. A constitution is the <u>supreme authority</u> of that organization. Laws are definitions, and it should be borne in mind that what we call <u>laws of Nature</u> are simply definitions and descriptions of the sequence of events in some particular field of <u>observation</u>. Thus it is highly important for the occultist and psychologist to understand clearly that our personal definitions (or naming) of the meanings of our experience and existence constitute suggestions which are accepted without reservation by sub-consciousness. Thus, in one sense, every man makes his own law, writes the constitution of his own personal world, and his life experience is the reproduction of that constitution through sub-consciousness. Take this statement literally, but not <u>too</u> literally. It is true only when you comprehend man as something more than a personality who is born, lives a few short years upon this sphere, dies, and vanishes forever.

The first of the twelve zodiacal signs, Aries, is assigned to the 4th Key. It is the first sign because it symbolizes the outgoing, ordered, cyclic motion, emanating from the Primal Will which is the beginning of cosmic manifestation. This sign rules the head and face and dominates the higher functions of the brain.

Aries is ruled by the planet Mars, which represents the fiery activity that is at work in the establishment of the universal order. It is, in man, the fiery desire nature whose dynamic energy is the "motivation of evolution."

The Sun is exalted (i.e. finds its highest expression) in Aries. We may understand from this that the highest manifestation of solar energy in our world is that which is expressed in those functions and powers of man which are ruled by Aries and symbolized by Key 4, viz., transformation in the human brain. Of all of the mechanisms, or organisms, on the face of the earth, the brain of man is the <u>most powerful</u>. The brain is run by solar force, as is every other bodily organ. Strictly speaking, the brain does not transform solar energy into thoughts. What it does is to transform this energy into <u>rates of vibration</u> which enable the personal consciousness to <u>receive</u> the ideas which, already inherent in the Universal Mind are continually being broadcast throughout all space. The principle is similar to that used in radio where an electric current in the receiving set establishes vibrations which can be attuned to the broadcasting station. The receiving set does not make the music. Neither does the brain make the thought. The brain simply provides the necessary conditions, as does a receiving set, whereby thought can find expression.

The head and arms of the Emperor form a triangle while the position of his legs suggests a cross. Thus he forms the geometrical figure shown in the margin. The triangle represents Light, and is the symbol of the Creative Spirit. The cross represents Life and Action and is a symbol of the physical plane (number 4). As they are combined they represent the alchemical SULPHUR, which is identical with the fiery desire nature.

The golden helmet is surmounted by the conventional astrological symbol of Aries. It is ornamented by twelve points, six of which are visible. The space between the bars is red, so that the colors, gold and red, are those of the Sun and Mars, the two planets active in Aries.

The sceptre is a modified Egyptian cross, combining the circle and Tau, which are symbols of feminine and masculine modes of Life expression. It is of gold to represent solar energy. The globe and cross, except for color, has a similar meaning to that in the hand of the Empress.

The armor of the Emperor is of steel, symbolizing the added strength obtainable from the intelligent use of iron, which is the metal of Mars and symbolizes the Mars force in the human personality. It also indicates protective power.

The skirt of the armor and flaps that cover the arms are of royal purple. This shows the combination of objective (red) and subjective (blue) mental activities. It is this combination that makes the Emperor royal and able to rule.

The cubic stone has been explained in the lesson on the High Priestess, since it is the same as that upon which she is seated. The ram's head is a reference to the sign of Aries, which is represented in astrological symbology by a ram.

The mountains in the background are of igneous rock, which is red to emphasize the fiery quality of the sign Aries. These barren peaks are in sharp contrast to the fertility and productiveness of the Empress' garden. They represent vividly the barrenness of mere intellection, use of the reasoning faculty for the sake of its use with no direct application to life. They also represent the sterility of mere regulation and arrangement unless there be something warm and vital to set in order.

The 4th Tarot Key is intended to impress upon you a clear pattern of the ruling power of consciousness. Whenever you exercise true reason, whenever you interpret an experience correctly, whenever you frame a satisfactory definition you are actually using the power that defined and framed the universe and which eternally rules it. That power, at work in you, is the maker and framer of worlds, and the maker and framer of your personal world. IT RULES EVERYTHING NOW. AT THIS MOMENT, AND ALWAYS, IT HAS ABSOLUTE COMMAND OVER EVERY CIRCUMSTANCE AND CONDITON.

The message of this Key has nowhere found better expression in words than in the last two stanzas of Angela Morgan's beautiful poem, The Cosmic Fire:

DUST! Why, the Future laughs at our dull sight;
  Laughs at the judgment linking man to sod –
    Damning him ever with decay and blight
    When at his center burns the blaze of God!
    The Force that flung the far suns into space
    Pushes and throbs through an eternal plan;
  The Mind that claims the singing stars in place
    Implores fulfillment in the soul of man.

O GOD, give us the whirlwind vision! Let us see
    Clear-eyed, that flame creation we call earth,
    And Man, the shining image, like to Thee.
    Let the new age come swiftly to the birth,
When this – <u>Thy</u> world – shall know itself divine;
  And mortals, waking from their dream of sense,
    Shall ask no proof, no message, and no sign –
    Man's larger <u>sight</u> the unanswerable evidence!

INTUITION

By this time you will have become used to a definite method of studying these lessons which you will follow throughout the entire series. First meditate upon your Tarot Key for five minutes. Then study the lesson, reflect upon it as you read, and write any observations into your diary.

Read the meanings of the number 5 in lesson 2. Note that this number symbolizes the <u>results</u> of the classifying activities in Key 4. A <u>subconscious</u> elaboration of these classifications, and the formulation of <u>deductions</u> therefrom which are projected back into self-consciousness, are the mental states termed <u>intuitions</u>. Note the cyclic action of this process. Every idea thus projected into self-consciousness is another suggestion to sub-consciousness, which is the start of a fresh series of deductions. The working out of this process may be instantaneous. This is what happens when we "think rapidly," as most people express it. On the other hand it may be a matter of days. A common example of this, and one which you have probably experienced many times, is when you read a difficult passage in a book which is very obscure at the time, but which is perfectly simple and clear the next time you see it, even though you may not have given it conscious attention in the interval.

Intuition means "interior teaching." As here treated, intuition is understood as being direct perception of the eternal principles which may be applied to the solution of human problems and human control over Nature. This direct perception is the result of the UNION of personal consciousness with the Super-conscious I AM, or the Central Self of every one of us. Such perception makes a human being immediately aware of these eternal principles, but it does not stop there. Included in this awareness is also a perception of the way in which the principles may be put into practice. There is a distinct difference between intuitions of this sort and those which are rooted in the personal sub-consciousness. This latter type is closely related to what are commonly called "hunches." Intuitions which originate in Super-consciousness may be correctly termed "Spiritual Intuitions."

The most important word in the last paragraph is union. Unless there is a real union between the personality and the true Self, there can never be an expression of Super-consciousness and the man can never touch the high plane of spiritual intuition. This idea of union is symbolized in many ways by Key 5.

The Hebrew letter Vau (pronounced "waw") means "nail" or "hook." Both meanings symbolize union, since nails are used to join the various parts of a house together, and a hook joins an object hanging upon it to the foundation to which the hook is fastened. Notice that the idea of sustenance is directly connected with the ideas of nail and hook, since it is by means of nails that the house is sustained and a hook is that upon which something depends. When the Inner Self is linked consciously with the personality, man gains first-hand knowledge that all things are sustained and depend upon the ONE SELF.

The idea of union is still further carried out by the primitive form of the letter Vau, which was simply a pictograph of a yoke, such as is used to harness oxen. Remember that the letter Aleph means "OX", and try to develop the hint contained here. The root of our English word "yoke" is the Sanskrit word "Yoga", the exact translation of which is "union." Yoga, as commonly taught, is a system of practices designed to bring about the complete union of the higher and lower natures of man. A similar idea is suggested by the word "religion" which means literally "bind together again." The religious doctrine of Atonement (at-one-ment) is another expression of the same idea. It is obvious that anything so deeply rooted in all of the world's religious must have some profound philosophical and practical basis.

The practical application of the idea of union is to be found in the function of HEARING, which is attributed to Key 5. It is not simply physical hearing that is referred to here, but to what is known as "interior hearing." Knowledge of the higher aspects of reality comes to us through the soundless sound of an Inner Voice, which often speaks as plainly as any voice heard with the physical ear. The reason is that the hearing centers of the brain, when developed to a certain extent, are stimulated by higher rates of vibration which serve as a means of communication between ourselves and more advanced thinkers.

Wise men throughout all the ages have taught and practiced union with the Life Principle, or One Self. Everywhere and always they have agreed that release from every limitation comes to those who awaken to a recognition of a power which is <u>always</u> present in human life, a power which sets men free when they know it and <u>use</u> it. That power is understood clearly only be those who have learned to listen to their voice within.

Geometrically number 5 is the pentagram. This figure is the symbol of Man, because 5 is the number of mediation (being the middle term between 1 and 10) and <u>Man is the Mediator between God and Nature</u>. Write the last part of the preceding sentence, which is underlined, in your notebook, and <u>remember it</u>. It is a key to many of the mysteries of Tarot.

Taurus is ruled by Venus and is the sign of the Moon's exaltation. Reflect upon this for a few moments and you will see that Intuition comes as the progeny of the Empress (Venus), who is the High Priestess (Moon), in her highest expression of active creation. This is one way of saying that the only way to contact Superconsciousness is through the subconscious mind.

The word "Hierophant" means literally "revealer of mysteries" or "he who shows that which is sacred." In the ancient Greek mysteries the Hierophant was the teacher who explained the meanings of the sacred symbols. Thus the Inner Voice represented by Key 5 will reveal to you the true mysteries of the Tarot and the inner or sacred meanings of its symbols. When this happens you will have not only a true understanding of the meaning of Life and its expression, but you will have a practical working knowledge of it. Again note that <u>explanation</u> is a linking process, uniting the knower with the known.

Like the High Priestess, the Hierophant is seated in a temple, in contrast to the Emperor, whose throne is out of doors. The Emperor wears armor, but the Hierophant wears the vestments of the peaceful priestly office. The insignia of the Emperor are those of earthly rulership and authority, while those of the Hierophant represent spiritual dominion.

The outer robe is red-orange, the color assigned to Taurus. It is trimmed with blue-green edging which is the complementary color of red-orange and refers to the sign Scorpio. The undergarment is blue like the robe of the High Priestess, and has a similar significance. Over this is the white robe of enlightenment. The outer robe is fastened at the throat (which is the part of the body ruled by Taurus) by a silver crescent, suggesting the exaltation of the Moon in Taurus.

The crown is similar to the triple papal crown. Note that it is egg-shaped, denoting that the One Force bestows spiritual sovereignty upon man, and that his life includes ALL THE POTENCIES OF THE UNIVERSE. The ornament hanging from the crown is a modified Yoke, referring to the primitive form of the letter Vau. It falls from the crown immediately behind the Heirophant's ears, to call attention to those organs of HEARING. The golden staff suggests the dominion of the Life Power through the planes of Nature, represented by the knob and three crossbars.

The golden keys suggest that an understanding of the power of Light (gold) unlocks the mysteries of life. Their wards show a "ball and clapper" design, denoting the importance of sound vibration and the faculty of hearing in the discovery of these mysteries.

The ministers who kneel before the Hierophant wear robes upon which are embroidered replicas of the flowers growing in the garden of the Magician, making the two figures <u>personifications</u> of the principles of <u>Desire</u> and <u>Knowledge</u>. This is to be understood that here these principles are manifest at the human level.

The throne, which is ornamented, and therefore a product of human adaptation, is of stone. The horned circles are variations of the conventional astrological symbols of the sign Taurus.

The pillars are of gray stone, and represent polarity. The ornamentation at the top of each of them represents the union of masculine and feminine potencies.

The background is gray, a color associated in occultism with Wisdom. It is a balanced mixture of black and white, another suggestion of the union of spirit and matter, the known and the unknown.

This week give attentive consideration to what goes on in your mind. You will find that most of your thinking is in words uttered by the inner counterpart of your own voice. But if you meditate faithfully upon the meanings of your Keys, asking direct, well formed questions in relation to them, you will occasionally receive impressions that have a different quality than your usual thoughts. It is as though somebody else were the speaker, and this is actually the fact. You simply put yourself in tune with other minds occupied with the same work that you are. Pay close attention to these thoughts which seem literally to come to you.

If they are constructive, encouraging, and illuminating, welcome them. If they are negative, DO NOT ATTEMPT TO REPRESS OR REJECT THEM. That is the wrong method of trying to control the mind. Resistance and repression simply divert the current of negative impression into subconscious levels. Instead of resistance, try readjustment. Remember that it is your own rate of mental vibration that determines what you receive from other centers of Life activity. You have the power to tune in on whatever you sincerely desire to receive. You can raise your mental rate of vibration by looking at Key 5. This will automatically cut off undesirable mental imagery by tuning it out.

The basis of the practice with this Key is to <u>relax,</u> to close your eyes, formulate a specific question, and visualize the picture of the Hierophant. LISTEN for your answer. <u>If it does not come in a few minutes, open your eyes and go about your business</u>.

But while you sit with your eyes closed do not speculate about the answer. LISTEN QUIETLY. Please remember that at all times such "listening" must be the alert, positive, and controlled responsiveness to the "still, small voice." Nothing negative or even remotely approaching "mediumistic" states is recommended. Never attempt to force the answer.

True intuition unfolds <u>principles,</u> not merely expedients. It is always concise, clear, and the meaning is unmistakable. True intuition never flatters, more likely it will reprove. True intuition never misleads and can stand the most severe spiritual, moral, and intellectual tests.

Therefore, TEST EVERY MESSAGE THAT COMES TO YOU THROUGH THIS CHANNEL OF INTERIOR HEARING. Test it for its ethical quality. Test it for reasonableness. Intuition often goes <u>beyond</u> reason, but it is never contrary to reason. Test it also for definiteness. The guidance which comes through intuition always has to do with special and particular applications of <u>eternal principles</u>.

This is why Lao-tze says: "Its counsel is always in season." If a voice speaks in your inner ear, and utters great promises of what you are going to accomplish in the future, or gives long discourses about unverifiable details of your former incarnations, or sonorous generalities, keep your poise. Very likely that is no more than your own sub-consciousness, dramatizing your wishes, or elaborating some promise of your conscious thought. The true inner voice gives counsel in season, when you can actually carry it out.

Sometimes the counsel is very simple. It says, "Do this", and what you are told to do may not seem to be of any particular moment. ALWAYS OBEY SUCH INNER ADMONITIONS, unless, as before explained, to do so involves some obvious breech of good sense or some violation of ethics. You will find that such obedience always leads to something of value. And the more you obey, the more guidance you will have.

Whatever really comes from the true Inner Voice is always something that illuminates, that leads to happiness and liberation, that makes for growth and development. Sometimes we hear voices utter messages full of gloom, full of portents of disaster, full of subtle promptings of spiritual pride and selfishness. But our test is simple. Is it the message of light and gladness? Then we may be sure it comes from the true Voice.

DISCRIMINATION

Contrary to our procedure in the previous lessons of this course of instruction, we shall consider the meanings of the Hebrew letter Zain before we go into those of the number 6. We do this for the reason that the meanings of the number grow out from, and are dependent upon, certain other meanings of the symbology of Key 6, as you will perceive directly.

In Hebrew the letter Zain (pronounced "zah-yin") means SWORD. Among other things the sword is an instrument of <u>cleavage</u>, something which is capable of making sharp divisions. This refers to a human faculty which the Hindus call BUDDHI. It is the <u>determinative</u> or <u>discriminative</u> faculty, the power to perceive <u>differences</u>. It is this power that is at the root of self-consciousness, since it is only with the self-consciousness mind that things are <u>perceived</u> as many apparently unrelated parts rather than as a single UNITY.

Note carefully that the MANY are only <u>apparently</u> unrelated. Buddhi is the power which makes things and conditions <u>seem to be real in and by themselves</u>. Yet these seeming realities are but reflections of the ONE REALITY in the universal sub-consciousness. The occult teaching is that all such reflections, i.e. everything, which changes, and is impermanent, is illusion, and therefore unreal. Since it is the attention of self-consciousness to particular ideas that acts upon sub-consciousness to bring those ideas into active manifestation, this power of being able to perceive differences, that is, to <u>create illusions</u>, is a fundamental necessity in order that individual self-consciousness might have existence. Otherwise all would be undiffused substance, unperceived by anyone, and hence, in effect, <u>without existence</u>, but only subsistence.

You will avoid confusion as to how self-conscious perception is the thing that makes self-consciousness possible if you will remember that manifestation is simply the way the ONE IDENTITY appears to ITSELF, and the instrument of ITS <u>Self perception</u> is that which is the faculty of self-consciousness in man. As the Book of Tokens puts it, "For the sake of creation the One Life that I am seemeth to divide itself, becoming Two." This division is called <u>superior</u> nature and the <u>inferior</u> nature. Though they are termed superior and inferior, each is equally as important as the other, for the superior nature is that which we are considering in this lesson as <u>Buddhi</u>, represented also by the Magician, while the inferior nature is the universal subconscious matrix upon which the superior nature acts, represented by the High Priestess.

Discrimination becomes most valuable to man when he uses it to perceive the difference between the real and the unreal. As long as he is a slave to appearances he perceives unreality, but when he begins to awaken from the dream of sense to the inner knowledge of his true nature, then he begins to understand reality. The Tarot pictures reality in terms understandable to sub-consciousness. It tells man the truth about appearances. Hence the intelligent study and contemplation of its symbols constitutes a phase of right discrimination. It is a distinct method whereby you turn from the unreal towards the real.

The number 6 means RECIPROCATION. Reciprocation is the act of giving and receiving mutually. You now see why a discussion of discrimination precedes that of reciprocation. Reciprocation is a relationship between distinct and separate parts. As it is to be understood here reciprocation is the relationship existing between the self-conscious and subconscious phases of mental activity, for the self-conscious mind gives suggestions which sub-consciousness receives, works out, and gives back to self-consciousness.

Reciprocity between opposites, when it is harmonious, is always of the same nature as that which we call LOVE. An inharmonious relationship is akin to HATE, which is the inversion of Love. Both love and hate are human emotions, but an eminent Master of occult wisdom once made a statement to the effect that they are spiritual emotions. This means that these are really root emotions, and that all other emotions and desires take on the character of either one or other of them. The Bible says that God is Love; hence we perceive that we approach God through the emotions and desires that have the attractive, beautiful character of the primal Love impulse rather than the selfish and separative motivation of hatred.

A moment's thought will make clear why this is so. If both emotions are spiritual they must alike be immortal. When cosmic manifestation occurs the process of involution takes place. This process is the separation of the One Thing into many parts. The force of Hatred in involutionary, and properly belongs to that phase of manifestation. But we as human beings are upon the path of return, or in

73

process of <u>evolution</u>. In other words we are headed back toward Unity. Consequently the force we must employ is the synthesizing, attractive force of Love, and our desires and emotions must be colored by that force. It is always a uniting force of great power. We utilize the separative faculty of discrimination, which we have already developed, to enable us to understand the illusive nature of separateness, and to enable us to determine the true color of our emotional life, and Key 6 tells us that it should be colored by emotions akin to Love.

The title, THE LOVERS, brings out the fact that <u>pairs of opposites</u> are not antagonists, but <u>complements</u>. The lovers are not simply the man and woman in the Key, but represent all opposites. Thus the main lesson to be drawn from the title is that right understanding of the universe shows it to be, in all of its details, an expression of the power of love, as the right and balanced relationship existing between the seeming many parts of which the universe is apparently made up.

The astrological attribution of Key 6 is to the zodiacal sign Gemini, the Twins. Here again you see the same symbolism of discrimination and separateness, and this is accentuated by the astrological symbol for this sign, which is II. This symbol also brings out the fact that opposites are really different aspects of one thing, just as heat and cold are different aspects of something we call temperature, past and future of that which we call time, and so on.

The planet Mercury rules Gemini. This planet is represented in Tarot by the Magician. Here again you see self-consciousness is the phase of consciousness which utilizes and controls the faculty of discrimination for the acquisition of knowledge and understanding of the true meaning of our conditions and environment.

The angel represents Super-consciousness. Thus he is the same as the Fool. He is shown resting upon clouds, indicating that the powers and activities of Super-consciousness are partly hidden from us because we have not yet developed to the point where we can penetrate the veil that keeps us from experiencing it. Nevertheless the influence from Super-consciousness flows down upon us, whether we recognize its presence or not.

He is also the archangel of Air, Raphael, which explains his yellow skin, since yellow is the color attributed to the element Air. His hair is red, yellow and green, colors of the plants Mars, Mercury and Venus. This suggests that one of the most valuable applications of discrimination is in the selection of the desire motives (Mars) to which attention (Mercury) is given, the results of which are manifested in our mental imagery (Venus).

The violet robe is the color of royalty and dominion, which is the function of Super-consciousness. The wings are red, to indicate the right discrimination leads to right desire, which expresses itself in right action.

Above the angel is the golden Sun, symbol of enlightenment. It shows that all conscious activity is a manifestation of the same ONE FORCE that comes to us as solar energy. It is this same Force which is differentiated into all pairs of opposites, from the highest to the lowest.

The man is self-consciousness, and corresponds to the Magician. He looks towards the woman, for he cannot see the angel himself. Only in her eyes can he catch a glimpse of the higher Being. This is a profound truth, for we do not come into direct contact with Super-consciousness with the Self-conscious mind. Instead we perceive it as reflected in the mirror of sub-consciousness. This does not mean, however, that we contact Super-conscious at second hand, for both self-consciousness and sub-consciousness are human modes of consciousness. This symbolism simply means that sub-consciousness is the means whereby we reach a state whereby we can comprehend Super-consciousness so that we can interpret it in terms of self-consciousness, but that the experience itself is entirely a subjective one. Hence the inability of anyone to make his Superconscious experience intelligible to anyone else who has not had a similar experience.

The woman is the High Priestess and also the Empress, and represents the subconscious level of mental activity. Both characters are nude to indicate that neither has anything to hide from the other, and that perfect reciprocal activity is possible only when the nature of each is entirely revealed to the other. Intelligent discrimination is possible only when all facts are revealed.

Behind the man is a tree bearing twelve fiery fruits. These represent the twelve signs of the zodiac and the twelve basic types of humanity. Behind the woman is a tree bearing five fruits. It is the tree of knowledge of good and evil, and the fruits represent the senses. This again brings out the attribution of discrimination to Key 6, since our most important discriminations are those between good and evil, and the senses are our means of making sharp discriminations on the physical plane.

The serpent coiled around the tree represents the fiery Serpent power, which is the basic force in human personality. This highly esoteric force will be dealt with at length in the lesson on Key 8. He is also the serpent of temptation of the Bible allegory.

The mountain in the background is a symbol of attainment and realization. It is the height on which the fool stands and also on which the Hermit is shown on Key 9. Its summit is reached from either the position where the man stands or from where the woman stands. The apex is where both paths meet and are blended into one. This, together with the purple color (a balance of red [masculine] and blue [feminine]) again reminds us that Superconsciousness is reached only by perfect interaction between self-consciousness and sub-consciousness.

This week keep a close watch upon your desires and impulses. Check up on your tendency to obey impulses without first submitting them to the light of reason. You will be surprised at the number of times that you perform inconsidered actions. Make an effort to discriminate intelligently between helpful actions and unimportant ones, between those that are purely selfish and those which reflect the influence of the unifying, harmonizing force of love. Be careful to discriminate intelligently however. There is entirely too much of the idea that in order for an impulse or desire to be good it must be unconcerned with personal happiness or pleasure. No bigger mistake can be made, for love expresses itself in happiness, pleasure, and well-being. Poor discrimination may cause some individuals to believe that happiness and well-being are concerned with selfish desires, but anyone who has developed a sense of "other-consciousness", or action with reference to others is under no such delusion.

Don't discontinue this practice at the end of the week. Make it a habit, and it will be the greatest help you have in the evolution and development of your character. Unselfishness and consideration of others is an absolute necessity before marked progress can be made upon the path of occultism.

WILL POWER

One of the most important meanings of number 7 is MASTERY. This means mastery over the personality and the conditions that make up environment. The power of WILL is the force that enables your real Self to exercise such mastery.

The occult conception of Will, however, is radically different from any other conception. <u>Will is in no sense a human faculty</u>. It is not something that strong-minded people possess and timid or so called weak-willed people are devoid of. Instead it is the living, motivating power behind the entire universe, and every person and thing in the universe has an equal share in it. Remember the affirmation of your Pattern number 0 which says, "ALL the power that ever was or will be is HERE, NOW." The difference between people is not the acquisition of greater amounts of Will power, but in their ability to express it more freely through their personalities.

The great mistake made by most teachers as to the nature of Will is that it is personal. As long as humanity suffers from the delusion that is has any will power <u>of its own</u>, just so long will it be held in bondage. It is even more absurd, if that be possible, than it would be for people to claim the air they breathe as their personal property, or as a personal attribute. Will is the power which man is able to express that frees him from blind fatalism.

It endows him with volition, the power to choose and discriminate.

While Will is above and beyond every human faculty, it nevertheless follows the development of the faculty of discrimination, or spiritual discernment represented by Key 6. Hence 7 logically follows 6 in the Tarot series. Will power cannot be utilized consciously without an inner discernment of its true nature. 6 stands for the process of equilibration. 7 is equilibrium, the result of 6, and it is the true secret of mastery. As long as we are buffeted about by the reciprocal activity of opposing forces instead of understanding how to balance their activity properly, we have not fully realized that ours is the victorious life.

Number 7 represents the diameter of a circle, because the ratio of the diameter of a circle to its circumference is as 7 is to 22, and the circle, the circumference of which is 22, has 7 for its diameter. The diameter of a circle is a line that connects its opposite sides. This is a graphic symbol of the fact that all opposites are in reality different aspects of one thing, just as the extremities of the diameter are but opposite points on one circle.

A circle circumscribes a definite area. This connects the meaning of the number with that of the Hebrew letter Cheth (pronounced approximately kayth) which means FIELD or FENCE. Both meanings imply the word ENCLOSURE. Primarily this field is the Universe, which includes all manifested objects and energies. In man the field is the personality, and the master, or cultivator of the personality is the true I AM, or Inner Self.

The idea of a field brings out the fact that personality is something which can be cultivated. That is to say, the potencies of Will power can be brought into active manifestation through the functions of a personality that has been properly prepared. Will power is the seed from which all possibilities are developed. It is also the fruition of these possibilities when they have been brought from latency into active manifestation. A little thought upon this idea will give you a flood of light upon the true purpose and function of the personality, and its value to man as an instrument for his own spiritual progress. But it must always be an instrument, never mistaken for a workman; always the field, never the cultivator. You are not your body, your emotions nor your intellect. If you were you could not apply the possessive case to them, for you do not possess that which you are.

A field is a definite, limited form. A word is a definite idea limited to a form that makes it intelligible to others. A word endows an idea with specific, definite meaning. Thus the human function of <u>speech</u> is attributed to Key 7. This refers not only to the spoken word, but to the unspoken language of thought. Thought always takes the form of words before it is intelligible to us.

Our habits of speech are the indices of our Will development. The words we use continually, every day, <u>and the meanings they have for us</u>, are the patterns of our life expression. This does not mean that people who use large and unusual words are expressing life more completely than those whose speech is simple and homely. Nine times out of ten such people do not know what they are talking about themselves, and if suddenly asked, "What do you mean?" would find themselves at a loss to make themselves clear. They are word gatherers, not word users. Do not use words unless you know what they mean. Use your dictionary faithfully and continually. An enriched vocabulary is a fertile source of mental imagery that is both broad and deep.

Accuracy in the use of words, care in the selection of words so that they convey true meanings, choice of positive, strong, courageous words – these are among the most important requirements for the development of the Will. Such words result in correspondingly positive mental, emotional and physical states, but their opposites result in despondency, confused thinking and ill health.

In occultism there are certain special word forms which are used in a very practical manner. These words have special vibratory power when they are spoken or sung. Such words are the mystic syllable AUM, the various Hebrew divine and angelic names, and certain other artificial sound combinations which are symbolic. The use of such special word forms is what the Hindus call Mantra yoga, which plays an important part of Will development. Such word forms are not to be experimented with by anyone who does not know what he is about, and not without the supervision of a competent teacher. Of the power of sound, Madame Blavatsky says in her Secret Doctrine that it is "a tremendous force, of which the electricity generated by a million Niagaras could never counteract the smallest potentiality, when directed with occult knowledge." Therefore, it is not exactly a plaything for people who want to see what will happen.

The zodiacal sign Cancer, the Crab, is attributed to Key 7. A crab is a shelled animal, hence has a direct relationship to the meaning of Cheth as a fence, and the meaning of 7 as safety and security. This sign is ruled by the Moon and the planet Jupiter is exalted therein. Our habitual subconscious mental states (the Moon) have definite rulership over our power of Will expression. The fact that the power of Will always expresses itself in some form of cyclic activity justify the exaltation of Jupiter in this Key. You will understand more about this when you come to the study of Key 10.

The title, The Chariot, relates to the letter meaning, since a chariot is a movable fence. Also it connects with the meanings of 7, and with astrological symbology, since it is a protecting shell, Cancer, which is a means of transportation, the Moon, which moves by rotations.

This Key is a graphic symbol of the constitution of man as individuality, or Inner Self, and personality, or outer vehicle. The rider is the true Self, and he wears the crown of the Primal Will and the wreath of Victory. He rides in the vehicle of the physical body, which is drawn by the sphinxes which represent the senses. These are guided by the reins of the mind, which are therefore invisible to the eye. The body is able to move by the rotational, vibratory activity of sunlight, the golden wheels, which is called in occultism Prana, or Ruach.

The crown of the charioteer is ornamented with three golden pentagrams. The pentagram symbolizes the dominion of the mind over the elements. They are five-pointed figures, referring to the faculty of spiritual intuition, Key 5, which a direct result of the expression of Will through the personality.

His fair hair is bound with a wreath, like that of the Fool, with whom he is synonymous. He is clad in armor, like the Emperor. The lunar crescents refer to the rulership of the Moon in Cancer. His cuirass is greenish-yellow to simulate brass, which is the metal of Venus, signifying the protection afforded by the right use of the power symbolized by the Empress. The square upon it symbolizes order and purity, while the three T's of which it is made up refer to the limiting power of Saturn, to which planet is attributed the Hebrew letter Tau. The skirt is divided into eight parts, and the units of design are geomantic symbols used in making magical talismans, or pantacles.

The sceptre is surmounted by a figure 8 which is combined with a crescent. This is a combination of the symbol over the Magician's head and the lunar symbol of the High Priestess. Thus the Charioteer's ensign of authority plainly indicates that his authority resides in the combination of self-conscious and subconscious activities.

The chariot, by its cubic shape and the material of which it is composed, which is stone, is the same as the thrones of the High Priestess and the Emperor. Four pillars, representing the four elements, support a starry canopy. The canopy represents the celestial forces whose descent into the physical plane through the elements is the cause of all physical manifestation. The shield on the face of the chariot symbolizes defense. The symbol upon it represents the union of positive and negative forces. The wings above it symbolize the element of air, which carries the power of the solar rays, represented by the golden orb between them.

The walled city in the background is clearly related to the fundamental meanings of the letter Cheth. The houses remind us of the letter Beth with its connotations of concentration and attention. The river, which flows behind the chariot, is the same stream of consciousness that began in the robe of the High Priestess. Trees growing on the river bank are of the same variety as those in the garden of the Empress, and symbolize the fertility of sub-consciousness.

Key 7 is the end of the first row of Keys in your tableau, and is the synthesis of all of them. It tells us that the chain of events leading to our ability to express Will power starts with the Magician. The acts of attention (Key 1) put to work the associative powers of sub-consciousness (Key 2) which results in the creation of concrete mental images and definite externalized conditions (Key 3). The observation and orderly correlation of these images, which present themselves to us as <u>facts</u>, is the faculty we call reason (Key 4). This enables us to test our intuitions (Key 5), with the result that we are able to make the discriminations between the real and the unreal, which, in turn, enable us to perceive the true nature of Will so that we can put it into practical application. The result is Victory, which brings security, safety and peace (Key 7).

This week spend some time in the deliberate attempt to realize that your Inner Self is something above and beyond your personality, something which is the true actor in your daily actions. Think of your personality as having no power of itself, but only that supplied by the One Will. This concept should become so habitual and natural that everything you say and do is influenced by it. In this way you will be taking an important step in the cultivation of your own personal field.

From now on pay more attention to your knowledge of words. If you have not been faithful in your use of the dictionary when you study, by all means use this important part of your practical work. Its value will be inestimable to you.

THE SECRET POWER

The Hebrew letter TETH (pronounced tayth) means snake. If you will study the form of the character in the corner of Key 8, you will see that the letter is simply a conventionalized picture of a coiled serpent. The serpent is one of the most frequently used and one of the most important in occultism. It has always been the favorite device of the Wise Ones when they wished to compress their knowledge of the GREAT MAGICAL AGENT into a single emblem.

The Great Magical Agent is an actual force that is used every day by everyone. It is cosmic electricity, the universal life principle, the conscious energy which takes form as all created things, and which builds all things from within. This force in the human personality is called Kundalini, or Serpent Fire.

Learning to control this Magical Agent is a part of the daily work of every student of Ageless Wisdom. One step in that control is the establishment of a clear intellectual perception of the truth that all of the varying forms of physical existence are merely transformations of this ONE energy. The world is full of a number of things, but they are all disguises of the ONE THING. The essential inner nature of the One Thing is SPIRIT.

The way to begin now to learn to control the serpent-power is to accustom yourself to think of everything as being a manifestation of <u>Spirit</u>. Perhaps you will be helped by thinking of everything as the direct expression of ONE RADIANT <u>MENTAL</u> ENERGY. It is a blind force only to those who fail to understand its nature. You must learn to think of it as a conscious, intelligent force. PRACTICE thinking this. Over and over again, as you look at things, <u>remind</u> yourself of their real nature. No matter if this idea is familiar to you; <u>make it second nature by repetition</u>.

In the average person the fiery power is dormant, or sleeping. It is a tremendous force, equally potent for destruction and debasement as it is for integration and illumination. It is a force not to be trifled with. No one should make an attempt to awaken it until he knows what he is about, for to do so is the most dangerous practice known to man. The ability to control it is only acquired after its nature is understood. The conditions under which it may safely be brought into activity are utmost purity of mind and desire, highest aspiration and ideals, and unselfishness in action.

Every attempt to build the above states within you results in a modification of your bodily organism. When your organism is sufficiently modified you will automatically be brought under the proper conditions for awakening the Serpent Power.

Now let us consider some of the reasons for calling this force the serpent-power. In Genesis we are told that the serpent was more <u>subtile</u> than any other beast of the field. The ordinary significance of the Hebrew word rendered <u>subtile</u> in the English version of the Bible is "cunning, dissembling, crafty." In addition to that the same word, with a slightly different vowel pointing spell the Hebrew adjective that means "naked, bare, uncovered."

88

Here is a reference to the essential nature of the Great Magical Agent. IT CONCEALS THE TRUE NATURE OF THINGS BY SEEKING TO EXPOSE THEM UN- COVERED.

That is to say that what we are calling the "Great Magical Agent" is that indefinable something which presents itself to us in various appearances. In each appearance it seems to show itself openly, without any concealment. But in reality every visible form is a <u>veil of concealment for a hidden truth</u>. Hence it is that those who call themselves "Realists" are often farthest from having any notion of the true reality. For them, appearances constitute the only truth. If they enter the field of art, they revel in what they call "naked truth," and their productions are usually characterized by emphasis upon the unpleasant details of appearances.

The true "REALIST" is he who is not taken in by the apparent openness of external conditions. He understands the subtlety of the serpent-power, and turns it into good use. Hence, in all ages throughout the history of mankind, great initiates have often called themselves and their pupils "Good Serpents." The Christian admonition, "Be ye wise as serpents, and harmless as doves," is an echo of this ancient custom.

The motion of the Magical Agent is serpentine. That is to say, it is wavy or undulating. It is a spiral force, yet at the same time it is vibratory. This motion of the serpent-power is the reason for assigning the number 8 to this Key, for 8 is the symbol of rhythm and vibration. To write it one begins at the top, and describes a letter "S", which is serpentine in form, and is the alphabetical symbol of a hissing sound. The movement is then continued, so as to form the reciprocal curves to those first described. Thus in writing the number 8 we make the same curved lines which are shown on the caduceus of Hermes by the two intertwined snakes. These are also the lines of the movement of the serpent-power within the human body. In this connection it is interesting to note that recent discoveries prove that lightning (one expression of the serpent-power) does not zigzag, but moves in sinuous curves.

8 is the only figure except 0 which can be written over and over again without lifting pen from paper. Thus it is a sign of endless and eternal activity, the Life Power in rhythmic, vibrating cyclic, spiral motion. In mathematics a horizontal figure 8 is the sign of infinity. In Christian occultism it is a symbol of the Holy Spirit, which has been described as a feminine potency. Hence the horizontal position in this connection. This is an esoteric conception with a world of meaning for the student.

Again, 8 is the symbol of the ancient teaching that all opposites are but effects of a single cause, and that a balanced reciprocal relationship between opposites results in the harmonious activity symbolized by the number. Indeed, the understanding of this is the secret of control of the Serpent-power.

In your tableau, Key 8 is the first of the second row of Keys, which, you remember, represents the laws, or agencies, whereby the principles represented by the Keys number 1 to 7 are carried into operation. Thus Key 8 represents the law which is the means of expression for the principle of attention which is represented by the Magician. That law is suggestion. It is by means of suggestions that the force concentrated by acts of attention is carried into manifestation for the modification of external conditions. Remember that the force so concentrated is the Love force, and you have the key to that which is the Secret of <u>All Spiritual Activities</u>.

The zodiacal sign Leo is attributed to Key 8. This sign is ruled by the Sun. In the human body it governs the heart and back. Among the tribes of Israel it represents the tribe of Judah, and this tribe had a Lion for its standard.

While the Ageless Wisdom is closely connected with the esoteric system of the Hebrew Qabalah, there has been but little said about it in these elementary lessons, because it is unwise to try to assimilate too much at one time. Nevertheless there are certain Qabalistic correspondences which are important in this connection, and we shall enter into them briefly there.

In Hebrew, the name of the sign Leo is Arieh (ARIH), and the letters of this noun are those which spell the noun RAIH, which means Sight. This faculty is that attributed to the letter Heh, and therefore associated with the sign Aries. The numerical value of these two words (216) is the same as that of the noun RVGZ which is literally translated "vibration." This word is particularly connected with the letter Samekh and the sign Sagittarius (Key 14). Leo, Aries and Sagittarius are what is known as the fiery triplicity in astrology, and hence have a close connection with the fiery activity of the serpent-power. Furthermore 216 is the number of the word GBVRH (Geburah) meaning "Strength." This is the name of one of the spheres of the Qablaistic diagram known as the <u>Tree of Life</u>. It is said to be the field of manifestation of the fiery planet Mars.

All of these Qabalistic correspondences point in one direction. They intimate plainly that strength, or working power is to be sought in a form of vibration which is fiery in quality, which is active in the sense of sight, and which is also connected in some way with the functions of the heart and back. This power is the light power that makes vision possible, and it is also the life power which is actually centered in the heart, and is the energy which carries on the prodigious labor of that organ.

Among the ideas suggested by the word LION are: rulership (since the lion is called king of beasts, courage, bravery, valor, resolution, tenacity, fortitude, will, decision, resolve). We say that a person who has these qualities has "backbone." Since resolution, courage and determination all imply self-control, the lion also represents self-mastery, self-possession, and self-reliance. It may be trite to observe that "God helps them who help themselves," but it is simply a common way of stating that the power of God (the serpent-power) is available to anyone who will prepare himself to utilize it and control its activity. "God is no respecter of persons," The Life Power is available to everyone, everywhere and all of the time, but it is only the "pure in heart" who see and understand the nature of the power of God.

The woman is the High Priestess, the Empress, and the woman in Key 6. She represents the subjective mind which controls the functions of every organ in the body, and directs the currents of Prana, or vital energy. The adjustment of the personality to the point where such direction brings about the modifications of bodily organism, to the extent that it is possible to affect a union with Superconscious levels, is directly dependent upon utilization of the law of Suggestion.

Like the Empress, the woman is fair haired and crowned, but her crown is of flowers instead of stars. The suggestion is that here we are concerned with organic processes rather than with the inorganic forces of crystallization represented by the hexagrams of the Empress' crown. Over head is the horizontal figure 8 that hovers over the head of the Magician, for she partakes of his influence, and represents the subconscious aspect of the same law he personifies. She is his working power.

The Empress sits but this woman stands, for the Empress represents the germination of mental images through subconscious responses to mental stimuli, whereas the picture now before us shows a more active function of the subconscious, namely, its control over every vital process, its direction of all the chemical activities of the body.

Her robe is pure white, like the inner garments of the Fool and the Magician. Thus this garment represents the purified aspect of sub-consciousness, which it assumes as a result of intelligent application of the law that is at all times amenable to suggestion. White also stands for the divine Unity, and is an emblem of regeneration, which results in a personal realization of the Oneness of All.

The chain of roses which goes around the lion's neck and encircles the waist of the woman forms a figure 8. Roses represent desire; hence the chain is a systematic series of desires woven together. Desires, rightly cultivated and combined, are the most potent forms of suggestion so that it is by definite formulation of desire, in harmony with the real nature of things, that we are able to dominate the mighty forces of nature below the human level of activity.

As the King of Beasts, the lion is the symbol of the highest forms of development in the kingdoms of nature below the human level. He is the ruling principle of the animal nature. He is also the alchemical symbol of one of the most important elements in the Great Work. That work is the transmuting of the gross elements of the natural man into the perfected man.

In alchemical works we hear of the Green Lion, the Red Lion, and the Old Lion. The Green Lion is the animal nature before it has been ripened and purified. The Red Lions is the animal nature brought under the control of the higher aspects of man's spiritual nature. The Red Lion is the lion of Key 8. The Old Lion represents a special state of consciousness which become manifest after the purification which produces the Red Lion. In that state of consciousness one becomes aware that the LIFE POWER is identical with the eternal RADIANT MENTAL ENERGY, which, because it WAS before anything else had been brought into existence, is, in time relations, older than anything else.

The scene is an open plain, in contrast to the city of Key 7. The suggestion is that what we are considering here is the operation of a law that is always at work throughout nature, and is not in any sense dependent upon the artificial conditions of man-made civilization. The law of suggestion is always at work. It is the primary law of sub-consciousness. No matter what external conditions may be, sub-consciousness is always dominant over the subhuman forces.

The mountain is the same as that which appears in Key 6. Mountains always represent causation, and are the abode of the gods in every myth. The Bible says that

Moses went up into the mountain to talk to God, and brought therefrom the Tables of the Law and the patterns of the Tabernacle. The same book tells the story of Jesus retiring often to the mountain to commune with the Father, and of his being transfigured on one such occasion. The mountain is the superior nature.

This week's practice work is highly important and you should make every effort to carry it out. The most valuable lesson you can learn is that of seeing through appearances and the consequent discovery of the inner Self. Whenever you have anything to do with another person try to keep in mind that it is not the appearance which you see that you are speaking or writing to. Remember that his inner nature is identical with yours, and <u>make the attempt to conceive of the real man</u>. This will be especially difficult in dealing with those who, for one reason or another, are unpleasant or repulsive to you. But make the attempt, anyhow, for that practice is more valuable than it would be in connection with someone you like. Don't make the mistake of being sentimental or emotional about it. This is an exercise in mental suggestion. Look deliberately for the good and beautiful in everyone, for that is an expression of the inner man. Don't gossip or discuss the unlovable things about anyone. Make the attempt to see everyone as perfect in reality, and you will help yourself by telling yourself the truth about all men and the power of your thought will be of great benefit to those upon whom it is turned. This exercise extends that of last week to include others as well as yourself, for the work of students of Ageless Wisdom must inevitably result in an understanding of the true meaning of Universal Brotherhood. It is a <u>fact in nature</u>, not a human emotional concept.

Pay particular attention to this lesson, for it deals with the force you are using for the regeneration of your personality. Use it and you will attain the heights. Abuse it, and it will destroy you utterly. It is Cosmic ELECTRICTY, of which Madame Blavatsky writes in her Secret Doctrine: "Mighty word, and still mightier symbol! Sacred generator of a no less sacred progeny; of fire – the creator, the preserver, and the destroyer; of light – the essence of our divine ancestors; of flame – the Soul of things."

RESPONSE

The law attributed to Key 9 is "Response." This law can be stated thus: EVERY ACTIVITY OF HUMAN PERSONALITY IS REALLY A RESPONSE TO THE INITIATIVE OF THE ORIGINATING PRINCIPLE OF THE UNIVERSE. The essential thought here is that no personal activity whatsoever has its beginning, source, or origin within the limits of the personality. All personal activity as derived reflected, responsive.

To every one of us it seems as though all of our thoughts and actions are the expression of purely personal motives. This semblance of personal initiative effects the most illumined of wise men, (except in rare moments of ecstatic identification with the Absolute) just as it does anyone else. But the wise man knows better and thinks differently from those who attempt to live upon the assumption that personal thought, feeling, and action are self caused.

Personality is the mask of the TRUE IDENTITY, and that IDENTITY is superior to, and unlimited by, the conditions of personality. It is from the inner and superior IDENTITY that all original impulse flows, and all of the activities of personality – the instrument or vehicle – are effects of this outward and downward movement of the energy, or working power, of the True IDENTITY or I AM.

The Ageless Wisdom teaches that there is but ONE IDENTITY in all of the universe, and every personality is but an expression of that ONE IDENTITY. It is the single source of all forms of existence. Its presence is the substance of everything. It is the energy of the ONE IDENTITY that is released in any particular form of activity. It is the mental quality of that ONE IDENTITY which is manifested in any particular expression of consciousness. Since your real nature is none other than that ONE, whatever laws and forces condition the activities of your personality must be laws and forces which proceed from your TRUE IDENTITY.

The Hebrew letter YOD resembles a tongue of flame in appearance. It is a component part of every letter of the Hebrew alphabet; it is because Yod is the foundation of the Hebrew letters that it is called the "Flame Alphabet." Since the Hebrew alphabet is, in itself, a symbol of everything that ever was or will be, it follows that the ONE IDENTITY, represented by Yod, enters into every mode of the Life Power's Self-expression.

Yod is a Hebrew word meaning "the hand of man." This is a clear indication of the ancient doctrine: THE PRIMARY AND FUNDAMENTAL REALITY OF THE UNIVERSE IS IDENTICAL WITH THE POWER WHICH FINDS EXPRESSION IN THE HANDIWORK OF HUMAN BEINGS. It is said of the letter Yod that is upper point represents the Primal Will, while the rest of it is assigned to the aspect of the Life Power called Wisdom. This means that all mental activity, which is the basis of all manifestation is derived directly from the ONE IDENTITY, is actuated by Its WILL.

Among the other meanings of this key is that of the <u>act</u> of contact, or union, or opposite forces. The hand of man is a vivid symbol of the potencies of contact of the higher with the lower, since it is the manipulator of instruments and that which creates instruments.

This Key represents <u>attainment</u> through <u>union</u>. This means that the end of the path is reached when the inner Self meets the personality in perfect union and contact. A graphic symbol of this is the slow, steady growth throughout the ages of stalagmites and stalactites in a cave. The stalagmite represents the personality and the stalactite the individuality. When at last they reach the stage of growth where they make contact, their united form is approximately that the letter I, which is the Greek and English form of the letter Yod.

In writing the figure 9 in ordinary script, the first part of the character is a reproduction of the Zero sign, and from the point where this circle is <u>closed</u>, a straight line, or figure 1, descends. In writing the circular part one describes a complete circuit, suggesting the completion of a course of action. Then the straight line is drawn, figure 1, which is the symbol of beginning. Thus the end of one cycle is always the beginning of the next. This is to show that attainment is never completed. After the union of the personality and individuality, which is the goal of human attainment, there are still greater heights to scale.

Nine, 9, is said to be the number of adeptship and of prophecy. It is easy to see how the Hermit represents adeptship, for he stands upon the mountain peak. His staff is in his left hand, which indicates that he does not need it for climbing. It is evident that he has reached the top, that he is supreme, that he has come to the end of the path of occult attainment.

It is not so obvious that he represents prophecy, although his white beard and venerable aspect suggest the traditional conception of what a prophet ought to look like. Yet the idea of prophecy is really represented by this picture. In the first place, a prophet is not merely one who makes predictions. If he is a true prophet his predictions must be correctly founded upon accurate knowledge, just as an astronomer predicts an eclipse hundreds of years ahead of time by his accurate knowledge of the principles governing astronomical movements. Hence a true prophet is one who understands the Law. He knows the principles upon which the self-expression of the Life Power is based. He has, so to say, been over the road, and this is what makes him competent to guide others.

The Hermit stands looking down over the path by which he has ascended, and which others are climbing. He knows every step of that path. He <u>foresees</u> all of the difficulties that the climbers will encounter. And this is something we need to keep remembering. For the Hermit, you recall, is the symbol of the I AM that is above every personality. Thus Tarot subtly intimates to us through this picture, that we are in continual contact with a Reality which already <u>knows</u> all that we have thought, all that we have done, and knows, also, every step on the path ahead of us.

This does not mean predestination, or fate, as generally understood. No outside force drives us remorselessly onward. Instead an indwelling Presence, timeless and eternal, knows already every experience we must go through in terms of time and space for the fulfillment of its purpose. It guides us, lovingly and sympathetically and sends the light of its omniscience into your personal consciousness to give us courage to continue the struggle against seeming limitation and bondage, which It <u>knows</u> are but appearances. Just as in the story of the Prodigal Son, the Father was waiting, and saw his son returning while yet he was far off, so does the One Identity seated in the hearts of men watch, from that pinnacle which is both above and within the personality, the approach of each soul toward the goal of true Self-realization.

The zodiacal sign Virgo is attributed to Key 9. Its ruler is Mercury. Virgo is the harvest sign, thus relating to food. The connection here is that Virgo rules the intestines, where food is assimilated and transmuted into bone, sinew, and tissue. At one stage of intestinal digestion, the food is transformed into an oily milky substance called chyle, from which the lacteals absorb nourishment for the bloodstream. When under proper manipulation, the <u>finer forces</u> always <u>present</u> in chyle are liberated into the bloodstream, they energize certain brain centers, and the result is a proper condition for illumination. And characteristic of illumination is the direct perception of the actual presence of the ONE IDENTITY.

It will pay you to pursue this thought as far as you can beyond this explanation. Consider the fact that in all of the legends of World-Saviors, the great one is always born of a Virgin. Consider, also, that Jesus is said to have been born in Bethlehem, which means "The House of Bread." The liberating power is born or released, in the dark cave of the House of Bread.

Mercury, which is the ruler of Virgo, and which is also exalted therein, represents the Life Power working at the self-conscious level, through the brain. This means that the highest expression of self-conscious activity is manifested in its control of the activities of the intestinal tract. This may sound strange, but it is perfectly true. We control the activities of the intestines from the self-conscious level by carefully choosing what we eat, and by utilizing the law of suggestion to bring about the release of the <u>subtle forces</u> in chyle.

This last seldom happens unless one knows of the possibility, <u>understands</u> to some degree <u>how</u> such release of subtle force will bring about illumination, and definitely takes himself in hand for the sake of accomplishing the Great Work. It has been said that God chooses the weak things of the world to confound the wise, and certainly the fact that illumination depends upon the release into the bloodstream of a subtle force that is generated in the intestinal tract is not one that will produce any feeling of pseudo-aestheticism. But there it is, a stubborn fact, and there is real beauty in it too, for those with eyes to see. For is not anything which contributes to illumination something that makes for the perception of true beauty?

The Hermit is he who stands alone, or he who is solitary. The ONE IDENTITY, because it <u>includes all</u> manifestation, is unique. It has no support other than Itself. Thus a certain book of Hebrew wisdom says that the letter Yod is "above all (symbolizing the Father) and with Him is none other associated."

He who stands alone symbolizes the adept, also, because, while he consciously identifies himself with all that is, by that very act he has set himself apart from the rest of humanity, because he cannot share his knowledge with those who cannot comprehend it. Thus he will always be, in a sense, a Hermit, by reason of his superior knowledge. This is not the prideful separativeness of the egotist, by any means. There was no tinge of egotism in Einstein's assertion that not twelve men in all of the world could understand his theory of relativity perfectly. Superiority and loneliness are inseparable. Yet the loneliness of the sage is not as the loneliness of the unenlightened, because the sage has what the less enlightened cannot enjoy, the constant companionship of the Supreme Self, the constant sense of union with that one Reality which is his own IDENTITY.

The scene of Key 9 is a direct antithesis of Strength. In the 8th Key we see a fertile valley, warmed by the Sun. Here is an icy, wind-swept peak, wrapped in darkness. This does not mean that they who experience the demonstration of the primordial glory receive naught for their pains but a sterile, icy perception of abstract truth. The Hermit, himself is warmly clad, and carries his own light. The cold and darkness are but symbols of the latency of the fiery activity of the ONE FORCE, and thus are in direct antithesis to the lion in the preceding Key. The heights of spiritual consciousness seem cold and dark for us, who have not scaled them; but they who stand upon those cold and lofty peaks suffer no discomfort.

The ice at the Hermit's feet is the source of the river in the Empress' garden, the same river that flows behind the Emperor and the Chariot. Here its power is arrested and crystallized, because the symbolism of this Key refers to THAT which does not, Itself, enter into action, thought it is the sum-total of all of the activity in the Universe.

The central figure is a bearded ancient. He is the "Most Holy Ancient One," identified in Qabalah with the

Primal Will. He is clad in gray, a mixture of black and white, the colors of the High Priestess' pillars, of the wand and rose of the Fool, and of the sphinxes which draw the Chariot. The Hermit has achieved equilibration, union of all pairs of opposites. His blue cap is in the shape of the letter YOD.

He has brought his lantern and staff with him from the valley below whence he came. The staff, a branch of a tree, is a product of the organic side of nature. It refers to the fiery activity, symbolized in Key 8, which he has used to help him on his Journey. Here he holds it in his left hand, to show that he no longer needs it for climbing.

The staff grew, but the lantern was made. It is of glass and metal, representing the inorganic side of nature. The basic principles upon which our understanding of cosmic law is founded are discoverable in the physical and chemical laws of the inorganic aspects of matter as they have been modified by man. We rely, however, upon the Life Power's self expression through organic beings to assist us in our efforts to rise above self-conscious limitations to the heights of Super-consciousness.

The light in the lantern is from a <u>six</u>-pointed star. This star is composed of two interlaced equilateral triangles which, from time immemorial, have typified the union of opposites. One of the great Masters of the Wisdom once made a statement to the effect that "he who understands this symbol, in all of its aspects, is virtually an adept."

The picture of the Hermit tells us that above the merely personal level of our daily existence there is a real Presence which now IS all that we aspire to be. That Presence, however far off it may seem to be, however inadequate our definitions of it may seem to us, however shrouded in darkness and obscurity its real nature, is friendly and definitely helpful.

Comprehend it we may not. Touch it we can, and as often as we remember to do so. For only by an illusion are we separate from it. In truth it enters into every tiniest detail of our lives. Actively present in all that we think, or say, or do is the ONE IDENTITY, the Ancient of the Ancient Ones, the fundamental and sole WILL, whence all manifestation proceeds.

Key 9 has a direct connection with each of the Keys preceding it in the series. As the number 9, it is the end of the numerical cycle, and includes with itself each of the preceding numbers. For instance, the Hermit is connected with the Fool in many ways. He is the Fool after his reascent up to the heights from which he fell, thus symbolizing the successful termination of a complete cycle of involution and evolution. The Fool is young Eternal Youth. The Hermit is aged, experienced. Yet both are the same, for both youth and age are but appearances of the No Thing. It is at once the oldest and youngest thing in the Universe. It is ageless, sexless, and changeless, yet has all of the potencies and causes of all phenomenal activities.

This week try to establish a logical connection between Key 9 and each Key in the series preceding it. You will find this exercise of great benefit in your Tarot work, for it is essential that you learn to recognize the relationships existing between the various Keys. This is entirely a matter of practice, and though it seems very difficult at first, you will find that it becomes increasingly easy with practice. Be sure to make the attempt. Write what you discover in your diary notebook.

ROTATION

The number 10 is a combination of 0 and 1. In lesson 2 of this series of lessons is the statement that 10 symbolizes the eternal creativeness of the Life Power; the incessant <u>whirling forth</u> of the Self-expression of the Primal Will; the ever turning Wheel of Manifestation. Let us consider the meaning of this.

0 is the symbol of the One Force. 1 is the symbol of the point wherein the One Force concentrates itself. Upon this symbolism, review lessons 3 and 4. It is at this point that the One Force becomes <u>active</u>, and consequently is the point where <u>motion</u> begins. Regarding this initial motion, Judge Troward, has written the following observations:

"At this initial stage, the first awakening, so to say, of Spirit into activity, its consciousness can only be that of activity <u>absolute</u>; that is, not as related to any other mode of activity, <u>because as yet there is none</u>, but only as related to an all-embracing Being; so that the <u>only possible</u> conception of Activity at this stage is that of <u>Self-sustained</u> activity, not depending on any preceding mode of activity because there is none. The law of reciprocity, therefore, demands a similar self-sustained motion in the material correspondence, and mathematical considerations show that the only sort of motion which can sustain a self-supporting body in vacuo is a rotary motion, bringing the body itself into a spherical form.

"Now this is exactly what we find at both extremes of the material world. At the big end the spheres of the planets rotating on their axes and revolving around the sun; and at the little end the spheres of the atoms consisting of particles which, modern science tells us, in like manner rotate around a common center at distances which are astronomical when compared with their own mass. Thus the two ultimate units of physical manifestation, the atom and the planet, both follow the same law of self-sustained motion which we have found that, on a priori grounds, they ought in order to express the primary activity of Spirit. And we may note in passing that this rotary, or absolute, motion is a combination of the only two possible modes of relative motion, namely motion from a point and motion to it, that is to say centrifugal and centripetal motion; so that in rotary or absolute motion we find that both the polarities of motion are included, thus repeating on the purely mechanical side the primordial principle of the Unity including the Duality in itself." --The Creative Process in the Individual, pp. 29-30

Study this quotation carefully. It is full of meat. Build up in your mind an image of the initial whirling motion in the vast expanse of Limitless Light. The doctrine of Rotation is one of the most important in occultism, for it is the very embodiment of the principles of growth, evolution, action and reaction, and the reciprocal relationship between every pair of opposites. It contains the secret of the manifested universe, for you will note that here we are dealing with things in manifestation, the comprehensible, and not with the incomprehensible Absolute which is motionless, changeless, and attributeless. Do not confuse absolute <u>motion</u> with the Absolute, for absolute motion is so called here simply because it is Self-derived and Self-sustained, and therefore unconditioned by other modes of activity.

The Hebrew letter Kaph represents a hand in the act of grasping, or a closed fist. Close your fist and turn it with the palm towards you. Note how the fingers suggest a <u>spiral</u>. The activity of the One Force is not simply in its form. Thus, and only thus, is such a thing as growth or evolution possible. We return to the starting point, it is true, but always upon a higher plane than where we began. Recall what was said in lesson 11 about spiral activity.

The basic idea suggested by Kaph is comprehension, or grasp. As stated above, we are dealing in this lesson not with the Infinite, but with a law of the Finite, which is definitely within our mental grasp. What we are considering now is the series of manifestations which is finite, however immense it might be. The principle of rotation which is at work in the entire series is intelligible. We can grasp it. It can be comprehended. This law, which can be understood and <u>applied</u>, is best represented by a <u>Wheel</u>.

The title thus refers to the universal cyclic activity. But here we must remember an important thing. <u>All there is within the whole series of manifestations is but the expression of the limitless power of the Infinite</u>. Furthermore, all there is is but the SINGLE expression of that power. The whole procession of activities in the phenomenal universe <u>is itself a unity</u>. All things are One, or, as better expressed, "The <u>related</u> Many equals the One."

The title also refers directly to the planet Jupiter which is attributed to Key 10. Jupiter is called in astrology the

"Greater Fortune." In mythology Jupiter is the ruler of all the gods, and through their agency, of the destinies of man. So it becomes evident to the careful student that this title will suggest the power whereby we find that, which we are seeking the power that makes us partakers of every good and perfect gift. It is perfectly true that the spiral, cyclic activity as applied to man is the means whereby he progresses along the path that leads to enlightenment and union, making him the master of his fate and the captain of his soul. The spiral motion, expressing through his personality, manifests as growth.

Jupiter is the planet that rules the astrological sign Cancer, which we have already considered in the study of Key 7. Thus the wheels which move the Chariot along represent the law of Rotation in that Key. A review of Key 7 should help you to see some of the practical applications of this law in your own life. When we <u>comprehend</u> the truth that even the <u>least</u> of our personal activities is a particular manifestation of some greater cycle of universal energy we shall find that every detail of those activities is adjusted harmoniously to the sweep of the currents of cosmic manifestation. Such comprehension gives man power over every disease, every misfortune, every limitation. The power of Jupiter, the Father, is <u>his</u> power. But it must be true <u>comprehension,</u> not merely an intellectual grasp that whatever we do is a part of the cosmic flux and reflux. It must be a realization, and that is arrived at by continually suggesting the idea to sub-consciousness by deep thought and by looking at the Tarot Keys, so that it automatically becomes a part of your mental makeup.

Jupiter is often called the "Sky Father", and thus the god of cloud, rain, lightning and thunder. This is close to what modern science has to say as to the nature of physical things. Whatever exists is a form of the manifestation of the electric energy pervading the atmosphere. It is the circulation of that energy that produces all forms. Here, also, we have the combination of the fiery energy which is the symbol of self-consciousness, and the water symbolism of sub-consciousness. All of these meanings are symbolized by the clouds in this Tarot Key.

The four figures at the corners of the Key are called the Cherubic emblems. They are the Cherubs mentioned in Ezekiel and in Revelation. They represent the Divine Name, IHVH, usually translated "Jehovah", which has an occult correspondence with Jove, or Jupiter. They also represent the fixed signs of the zodiac and the four elements. The Lion is Leo, and the element of fire. The eagle is Scorpio, and the element of water. The Man is Aquarius, and the element of air, while the bull represents Taurus and the element of earth. Thus they represent the fixed principles which remain unchanged throughout the cycles of manifestation.

The symbol of the wheel, as shown here, is taken from a diagram drawn by Eliphas Levi, which he called the "Wheel of Ezekiel." It is composed of three concentric circles. The innermost has eight spokes, and is thus the same as the wheel design on the dress of the Fool. It has the same general meaning, as a symbol of Spirit, or the Life Breath, and its whirling motion. The particular meaning here is that the first requirement for an adequate comprehension of existence is the perception that everything in the phenomenal world is an expression of Spirit, pervaded by the pure consciousness of Spirit, made of the substance of Spirit, and moved by the energy of Spirit.

The circle surrounding this innermost one is also divided into eight parts. It represents the activities of the formative world of the Qabalists. It contains alchemical symbols of Mercury, Sulphur, Salt, and Dissolution. The first three of these represent wisdom, activity and inertia respectively. These symbols represent the laws, or agencies, which carry the ruling power of Spirit out into manifestation, and which give man dominion over the powers of nature. Dominion is expressed through the combination of the three principles in the Great Work of dissolving all seeming obstacles by right knowledge, or true comprehension. This dissolution is what makes available for human use the energy locked up in form.

The outer circle contains the Roman characters ROTA. Read in this order they spell the Latin word for "wheel" but they may be recombined to form the words "ROTA TARO ORAT TORA ATOR." This sentence, (which is not good Latin) may be translated to mean, "The Wheel of Tarot speaks the Law of Hathor." Hathor is mother Nature, the Empress in Tarot.

These Roman characters are counterchanged with the four Hebrew letters, Yd He Vau He (IHVH), which is commonly translated Jehovah. Observe that the Roman letters are read clockwise around the wheel, as is shown by the position of the letter R. The Hebrew letters, on the contrary, are read in the opposite direction, and this is true with the reading of all Hebrew words. This is interesting, since it denotes a double movement. The suggestion is similar to that indicated by the horizontal 8 over the heads of the Magician and the woman in Strength.

The wheel is orange to indicate the fact that the power at work throughout nature is the same as that which comes to us from the suns as sunlight.

The serpent on the descending side of the Wheel is yellow to represent light. Its wavy form denotes vibration. It is a symbol of the descent of the serpent-power (Key 8) into physical existence, of the involution of light into form. It is the power which flows through the Magician, and is also the light in the Hermit's lantern.

The ascending figure is a Hermanubis, having the head of a jackal and the body of a man. It represents the type of evolving life which has reached the average human level at the present time. The animal head shows that humanity, as a whole, has not risen above the purely intellectual level. But his ears rise above the horizontal diameter of the wheel, showing that through interior hearing (intuition) man is beginning to gain some knowledge of the segment of the cycle of evolution through which he is destined to rise. This figure is red to denote self-consciousness and desire.

The sphinx represents the completion of the identification of the personality with the One Identity. She carries a sword, so that her weapon is that which the alphabet typifies by the letter Zain, signifying right discrimination.

The Sphinx is none other than the One Identity. In the old myth the answer to the riddle of the Sphinx was "Man." When we come to understand the true nature of man, we find that MAN is the REALITY which holds within Itself all that we commonly call Nature, even as Adam held Eve within himself before she was brought forth as a separate being.

Thus the sphinx, although she has a woman's head and breasts, has the hindquarters of a male lion. She combines the two principal elements in Key 8. She is the union of male and female powers, the perfect blending of forces which, at lower levels of perception, seem to be opposed. The figure is at the top of the wheel to symbolize stability, equilibrium, and balance in the midst of perpetual transformation, change and motion of the Universal process. It is super-consciousness, the attainment, the beginning of the end.

The law of Rotation is one of the most obvious in Nature. Yet it is one of the least understood. If humanity as a whole would realize that is future — not that of its children, but its very own future — is entirely dependent upon its present actions. Such a realization would mean the end of wars, of strife, of selfishness, and of all that tends to separate. It is important for you to realize the importance of this law. For that reason your exercise this week should be a studied attempt to see this law in operation. Begin by thinking of all of the things you can where cyclic or spiral activity is apparent. Then examine yourself. Think back over your past life, and note, if you can, the cycles through which you have passed. Think of your present activities, and try to picture their results in the future.

None of the forces in the universe is alien to man. The innermost reality in man is the One Identity behind, within, and surrounding the whole universe. This like the very center of the wheel is always at rest. Or, like the Sphinx, it remains unmoved throughout all the cycles of transformation. Grasp the truth behind this Key and you will find it a powerful weapon, a sword of right discrimination, enabling you to cut off all the forms of error and delusion which now bar your progress to complete liberation.

ACTION-EQUILIBRIUM

"Equilibrium is the basis of the Great Work", says an ancient occult maxim. This might also be termed the doctrine behind all of the meanings of Key 11. Consider the number itself for a few moments. Note that its digits equal each other. It is, in itself, a glyph of balance, of equilibrium. Thus the number typifies equality, balance, poise, etc.

The number 11 is somewhat similar to the sign of the zodiacal sign Gemini (♊) and the Roman numeral II. The idea of equilibration must have, for its root, the idea of duality. Balance is the result of equalizing two opposing forces or activities. Key 11 stands for that which the Hindus call "KARMA." This word is translated as "action (or work) and the fruit of action." Thus it invariably manifests itself as absolute, undeviating justice. Note well that equilibrium is not the cessation of action, not something static, but the constant, balanced, reciprocal action between pairs of opposites.

The Law of Equilibration, then, is the same as the Law of Polarity. Its application consists in the alternate use of contrary forces. Eliphas Levi says, "Equilibrium is the result of two forces, but if these were absolutely and permanently equal, equilibrium would be immobility, and consequently the negation of life. Movement is the result of alternated preponderance – warmth after cold, mildness after severity, affection after anger – is the secret of perpetual motion and the prolongation of power. To operate always on the same side and in the same manner is to overload one side of a balance, and the complete destruction of equilibrium will soon result. Everlasting caressing quickly engenders disgust and antipathy, in the same way that constant coldness or severity alienates and discourages affection in the end."

The same law is also stated in The Kybalion thus, "To destroy an undesirable rate of vibration, put in operation the Principle of Polarity and concentrate upon the opposite pole to that which you desire to suppress." The same book gives an excellent summary of the Principle of Polarity. It says, "Everything is dual; everything has poles; everything has its pair of opposites; like and unlike are the same; opposites are identical in nature, but different in degree, extremes meet; all truths are but half-truths; all paradoxes may be reconciled." Give a great deal of thought to these quotations because they set forth some very basic principles. They will do much to give you a clearer insight into the meaning of this Key.

Lay out your Tarot tableau as directed in Lesson two. Note the position of Key 11 in relation to the others. It is the pivot, the point where all the others balance. It is the very center of the Keys, the basis or hub of the wheel. So placed, it shows certain relationships which might ordinarily escape your notice. In the arrangement the Keys in the upper left-hand and lower right-hand corners are respectively 1 and 21. Their sum is 22, and since 11 is ½ of 22 it is mathematically the mean term, or middle number, between these extremes. In like manner 11 halfway between 2 and 20, and in the spatial arrangement of the tableau these two Keys occupy complementary positions <u>with ref-</u><u>erence to the 11 Key</u>. This is true of every pair of Keys the sum of which is 22.

At the present stage of your studies this fact is chiefly valuable to establish the fundamental meaning of Key 11 in your consciousness. But if you desire to work with these correspondences, it will be well to know that the Key bearing the lowest number is always the <u>active</u> term, the highest number is always the <u>passive</u> term, and Key 11 is always the <u>relationship</u> term; that is, the law or agency through and by means of which the active is directed upon the passive principle. Thus in Key 1 the active term is <u>at-</u><u>tention</u>. In Key 21 the passive term is limitation. The rela-tionship between them is <u>balance</u>. Thus <u>attention</u> directed upon a definite <u>limited</u> field of conscious activity through the agency of poised, <u>balanced</u> mind, emotions and body, brings about the state that enables us to affect the contact or union with the Inner Self which is the object of our work with Tarot.

The Hebrew letter Lamed (pronounced "law-med") means "Ox-goad." Thus it suggests the idea of control. The man who understands and applies the Law of Equili-brium has perfect control over all natural forces.

An Ox-goad is that which urges or incites an ox to <u>ac-</u><u>tion,</u> and keeps him on the road chosen by his driver. In Tarot the Ox is the letter Aleph, and, although it is not re-ally true that we incite the super-consciousness Life Pow-er to enter into activity, nor true that we in any sense con-trol or determine its perfectly free activity, nevertheless we seem to do <u>both</u> of these things. What really happens is that the Life Power directs itself through the functions of personal consciousness which are represented by the letter

Lamed; but so far as we are concerned those functions appear to originate within us, and thus all but those who are properly instructed naturally suppose these activities to be something peculiar to themselves. Control over the Life Force consists in attaining a state of equilibration where it can find free expression through our personalities. So, for all practical purposes, even those who understand the truth of the matter act just as if they were directing the Life Power, just as a man who knows that the sun does not revolve around the earth may, nevertheless, reckon the hour by its apparent position in the sky.

The shape of the letter Lamed is that of a serpent, so that it contains more than a hint that the force represented by this letter is the same as that discussed in Key 8. Note well, however, that while the letter Teth represents a coiled serpent, Lamed represents it uncoiled and active.

The zodiacal sign Libra is attributed to this Key. Libra means "the Balance" so that its attribution to Justice is obvious. It implies equilibration resulting from the action and reaction of opposites. In this sign Venus is the ruler and Saturn is in exaltation.

Venus, the Empress, you will recall stands for imagination. All books of Yoga instruct their readers in the use of imagination. The books of the alchemists abound in similar elaborate imagery, which has the same use. Modern metaphysical and advanced thought teachers have made extended use of the same principle. It is the foundation of all of the practical benefits of the Tarot.

Imagination builds faith. True imagination, and not mere fancy, rests on the firm foundation of science. The Arabian Nights gives us a fanciful idea of the idea of flying in the story of the Magic Carpet. But from Leonardo de Vinci to the Wright Brothers, true creative imagination has been busy with the problem of aviation. With every advance in exact <u>knowledge</u>, clearer imagery became possible, and with clearer imagery came firmer <u>faith</u> that human beings would eventually fly. Leonardo had his faith, although he never succeeded in flying. So he collected facts and classified them, and made a real contribution to the science of aviation. But the Arabian spinner of fairy tales was content with mere fancy. Therefore he had no service to give along the lines of scientific aviation, for he had no real faith in the idea of human flight.

Faith is a prime requisite for the accomplishment of the Great Work. Without faith you can do nothing. You must have confidence in the principles by which you operate. You must have faith in <u>yourself</u>. This is one reason why it is customary in occult schools to make the pupil familiar with the lives of the Adepts who have achieved success in the Great Work. There are few better uses of your time than in the study of the lives of Jesus and Buddha, for in what they said and did we may find all the principles of the Great Work explained and exemplified.

Saturn, the planet which is exalted in Libra, is the power of limitation which produces all form. It is the active power at work in Karma, which expresses itself to us as undeviating justice. Hence it is the power which has its highest manifestation in the Great Work which enables us to control Karma. Man can make full and complete conquest of his future; he can make whatever Karma he chooses.

There is a lot of silly talk about Karma, and some people are so afraid of "making bad Karma" that they do nothing at all to improve the conditions under which they live. Others are afraid of interfering with Karma. It can't be done. They can generate fresh Karma, but they cannot change an immutable law, or interfere with it. Then there is the type of person who "invites his Karma," and immediately thereafter has all sorts of unpleasant things happen to him. The truth of the matter is that he has suggested the unpleasant consequences, and his sub-consciousness faithfully reproduces them in his environment. He has not called down his Karma; he has simply made some nice fresh Karma for himself.

As a matter of fact there is no escape from Karma. There is really no such thing as inaction in all of the universe. The fruit of what we call inaction is loss of faculty and function, for that which is not used atrophies. But that very loss of power is action in the wrong direction. Madame Blavatsky says, "Inaction in a deed of mercy is <u>action</u> in a deadly sin." The truth of the whole matter is found in the admonition, "Whatsoever thy hand findeth to do, do it with all thy might." This does not mean that you should exert as much force in picking up a pin as you would use to lift a crow-bar. "With all thy might" means that you must apply your whole power to whatever you do, whether the <u>degree</u> of power be small or great. To do this takes concentration, and concentration is basically <u>limitation</u>, or the elimination of every distraction which take force away from the work you have at hand. This is why the Great Work is connected with the sign which represents the exaltation of Saturn, since it is the saturnine power of concentration that is used in all stages of the operation.

"Justice," said Omar Khayyam, "is the soul of the universe." The Woman in Key 11 is identical with the Empress, who is indeed the "soul of the universe." She is creative imagination, and the power of sub-consciousness to produce perfect equilibration throughout the organism. She also represents the rulership of Venus in Libra.

Her crown is surmounted with a triple ornament, which is in accordance with the esoteric version of this key. It represents the serpent-power in its highest manifestation, which releases human consciousness from its three dimensional interpretation of the universe. The circle and square on the front of the crown refer to the movement of Spirit within matter. Thus it is similar to the symbolism of Key 10, which shows the wheel surrounded by the four cherubs.

The ornament of the breasts of the woman is an elipse encircling a T-cross, thus containing the mathematical elements that enter into the construction of Key 21. Key 21 represents Saturn, the measuring power, so that the T, which is a measuring tool, is colored blue-violet, color of Saturn in our color scale.

The pointed blade of the sword has the same basic meaning as the ox-goad. It is of steel, metal ruled by Mars, and this is a reference to the fact that wherever the Venus activity which rules Libra is called into play, the Mars force is active also, because these two are complementary and the operation of one invariably excites the operation of the other. The sword handle is in the form of the letter Tau, so that the uplifted sword is a symbol of the exaltation of Saturn in Libra.

The cape is green, referring to Venus, and also to the color of the sign Libra. The robe is red, complementary to green, symbolizing the Mars force mentioned in the preceding paragraph.

The scales represent weighing and measuring. They are, of course, closely related to the basic meanings of this Key. Note that as an instrument for measuring they again refer to the influence of Saturn in this Key.

The background and curtains illustrate the Law of Polarity by their contrasting colors. The background is yellow, the color attributed to Air. The curtains are violet, which is complementary to yellow. Violet is the color attributed to Jupiter, and the curtains refer to the mechanism of cosmic activity represented by the Wheel of Fortune, because that mechanism to some extent veils the operation of the Life Breath. The symmetrical arrangement signifies balance. Their folds are reminiscent of the drapery of the robe of the High Priestess, and have the same meaning.

The throne repeats the symbolism of the pillars and veil of the High Priestess on a smaller scale. Here the pillars are part of the throne, and are surmounted by pomegranates instead of lotus buds, to show that in Key 11 the activity represented has arrived at fruition.

This week consider your actions more carefully than you have ever done before. Try to keep in mind that your present actions are the basis of your future conditions. Go about your daily tasks earnestly, no matter how trivial they may seem. It is not the size or importance of the action that counts, but the manner of its accomplishment. No one ever did great things well who had not first done small things well. Do not misinterpret this to mean that you should drive yourself unmercifully. To do so is a wrong action, for you place a strain upon your mind and body, whereas you should care for them as diligently as you would any other fine animal that you expected to serve you faithfully and well. But the beginning of the solution of your problems is to understand the meaning of right action, and then to <u>act rightly</u>.

Go about your duties in a poised, quiet manner. When you sit down to study, sit quietly and perfectly still. Teach your body the meaning of balance. This is not only highly necessary training for an occultist, but it is the most potent suggestion you can give to subconsciousness that you wish it to set to work to equilibrate your entire organism.

Fear not. Be free from anxiety. Do not yield to the mood of haste. Whatever you have to do, try as best you can to realize that every activity is a particular expression of the perfect action of the Life Force. Look upon your desires as <u>present realities</u>. Thus counsel the Wise Ones.

REVERSAL

The symbolism of Key 12 is as obviously related to the Law of Reversal as that of Key 11 is to the Law of Equilibrium. The application of this law finds its expression in the completely reversed outlook of the truly wise from that of the ordinary man. For the person who is truly enlightened, who has truly identified himself with the One Identity, everything in his entire experience is reversed. No longer does he perceive the universe as a warring, separative multiplicity of things and conditions. He sees it instead as a unity which manifests itself as a succession of harmoniously related parts, none of which stands alone and all of which are sustained as the expression of that Unity in its entirety. No matter where he may be, no matter how things may seem, he is consciously aware that "all the power that ever was or will be is here, now."

The Hebrew letter Mem, (pronounced "maym") means waters or seas. In occultism it stands for the element of water. Water symbolizes the Law of Reversal, because it reflects everything upside down. More than that, however, the man who has truly made this important reversal of consciousness is alone able to understand what is really meant by the word "water" in occultism. Others may be able to grasp the idea intellectually, but he knows it first hand, and thus fully comprehends its significance.

We have already learned, in the symbolism of the High Priestess, to identify water with sub-consciousness. We also learned in the symbolism that sub-consciousness is actually the substance that is in every form in the entire universe, that One Thing from which all things are made. Consequently it will be easy to recognize the letter Mem as signifying the Mother Deep, or the Root of Nature. This is further carried out by the fact that this letter is one of the three mother letters of the Hebrew alphabet, Aleph and Shin being the other two. They are really representative of the three aspects of the Absolute, or the All.

In this connection there are many points of a highly metaphysical nature that might be brought out, but it is for students of metaphysics to ponder the obvious implications of this Key. This instruction is intended for practical use, so that, beyond an occasional hint, we shall abstain from highly metaphysical interpretations of the Tarot. This universal sub-consciousness is also your personal sub-consciousness. Its creative faculties are those which you govern and control through the suggestions given to it by your self-conscious mind. One of the things that makes all forms of mental and occult practice seem so difficult is the supposition that what we have to do demands the extertion of an intangible mental power against the inertia of a very tangible physical reality. This "matter" which surrounds us seems so dense, so resistant, so hard to move, that most people consider it preposterous to believe that mere thinking can have any power over it.

The occultist is not taken in by any such surface appearances. He sees himself surrounded by things which have neither the solidity nor the inertia that his unaided senses report. He understands that the densest forms of physical substance, as well as the lightest gases, are really forms of energy, built up from infinitesimal, widely separated drops of the fluidic "water" of the occultists. Thus, when he begins to attack the practice problem of changing conditions by changing his thinking he does not face the difficulty which besets everyone who believes what his senses report about the things in his environment. The practical occultist knows that there is no different between the energy which takes form as thought and that which takes form is a diamond, a piece of mental, or any other physical object. Furthermore, he knows that thought-forms are centers of more intense and more lasting activity than any physical thing.

Thus the occult teaching about water as substance, which is precisely the same, in many respects, as the modern scientific conception of the electrical constitution of matter, enables the aspirant to effect a reversal in his mental attitude toward the conditions of his environment. By means of this reversal he is enabled to free his mind from that subjection to appearances which prevents most people from using their thought-power to change conditions for the better.

For the student of occultism the number 12 is almost inexhaustible in its meanings. It is like the number 7 in that respect, and it is also related to that number. 12 is the product of 3 and 4, while 7 is their sum. We are already familiar with 12 and 7 as representing the number of signs of the zodiac and the number of planets respectively. 12 is associated with the idea of completeness, because there are 12 months in the year and 12 signs in the zodiac.

Since 12 is composed of the digits 1 and 2, (and we read digits from right to left) 12 expresses the idea of the manifestation of 2 through the agency of 1. In Tarot 2 is the High Priestess and 1 is the Magician, so that this reading suggests the outpouring of the powers of sub-consciousness through the fixation of attention.

This is precisely what the Hanged Man typifies. When concentration is prolonged, the effect produced is what the Hindus call <u>Samadhi,</u> or the <u>Super-conscious</u> state of existence. It is the perfect union of the personal consciousness with the universal, attained by practices which quiet the <u>mind,</u> and <u>suspend</u> the formation of association of ideas.

The title, "The Hanged Man", clearly refers to the result of these practices. Without changing its meaning, we might just as well call it the "Suspended Man." The Hindu word for mind is "manas," and our English word "man" is derived from the same root. Thus mind and man are essentially closely related ideas, so that this title immediately suggests to the initiated the idea of the "suspended mind" or the suspension of personal activity. This suspension is achieved by concentration. When concentration is prolonged, Samadhi is attained, and with it the release of those marvelous powers of sub-consciousness which give the adept perfect control over his mind, his body, and the conditions of this environment.

As a result of even momentary experience of the super-conscious state, one's whole attitude toward life is changed. The person who has had this experience feels himself to be merely a vehicle, or instrument of the cosmic Life Breath. Gone forever is the delusion that personality is, or can be, separate from the sum-total of universal activity. The words of Jesus, "Of myself I can do nothing," express the state of mind reached by all who have this experience. Yet this is not in any sense a confession

130

of weakness. It is simply the recognition that there is not the least personal activity which is not the expression of universal forces and laws. Instead of lessening the importance of personality, this consciousness tremendously increases it, for it shows that the real value of personality lies in the fact that it can act as the agency whereby the limitless powers of the One Life may be brought down into manifestation in the conditions of relative existence.

The planet Neptune is the astrological attribution of Key 12. This planet, although not discovered by exoteric astronomers when these Keys were invented, was nevertheless known about by occultists, so that we consequently find a place for it in the Tarot series. One has only to know that astrologers assign the quality of INVERSION to Neptune to connect it immediately with this Key.

Neptune is said to be the ruler of inspiration, psychometry and mediumship. It is also connected with the gases and drugs that produce unconsciousness. It is an established fact that many of these drugs and gases produce a bodily change that makes possible, for a short time, an imperfect perception of higher forms of consciousness.

Be on your guard here. You may have read of the many cases on record in which a narcotic drug or gas has opened temporarily the gateway of the higher consciousness. Never experiment with such dangerous things. No intelligent occultist ever uses drugs for that purpose. The reason is that although such chemical substances, when introduced into the blood, do bring about the action of the brain centers through which higher consciousness may be expressed, the active principle in them that produces this result cannot be separated by any process known to modern chemistry from certain other substances which are terribly dangerous.

Yet the fact that narcotic drugs can sometimes enable one to experience a measure of super-consciousness points to one conclusion. He who experiences the Divine Consciousness does so because of a chemical change in the composition of his blood. But this change must be effected from within the bodily organism, and not from outside agencies. Since the bodily processes are completely under the control of subconsciousness, it follow that the alteration of bodily states is also effected by subconsciousness. The necessary chemical change in your organism is most properly brought about by the kind of work you are doing in this instruction. When you look at these Tarot Keys and carry out the other directions given in these pages, you give subconsciousness certain definite patterns upon which to work. The response to these patterns brings about the modifications in your body chemistry in that perfectly normal and safe way. The ultimate result is that you will experience the kind of consciousness represented by Key 12.

The gallows is in the shape of the letter Tau, attributed to Key 21. Each upright line of the letter is a tree trunk having six, lopped branches. These stand for the powers symbolized by the 12 simple letters of the Hebrew alphabet, the 12 signs of the zodiac, the parts of the body governed by them, etc. Thus the gallows, as the letter Tau, refers to the Universe as a rhythmic "dance of life." From this the Hanged Man is suspended, as an intimation that super-consciousness brings a vivid realization that human personality is dependent upon, and adequately supported by, the totality of cosmic forces.

The legs of the Hanged Man form an inverted figure 4, which here refers to Reason. They are dressed in red to indicate the fact, often overlooked by tyros in practical occultism, that what appears to be inaction in states of intense concentration is really tremendous activity. The mind in the state of Samadhi is still, just as a spinning top is still, because it is moving with great rapidity in an unbroken flow of knowledge around a single point of consciousness.

The arms and head of the Hanged Man suggest the points of a triangle, so that the whole figure represents 4 by the legs and 3 by the arms and head, with 3 beneath. Now 3 and 4 are the factors of 12, and in Tarot 3 is the Empress and 4 is the Emperor. Hence this arrangement shows the subordination of imagination to reason. This is exactly the mental result of applying the Law of Reversal Most people permit reason to be dominated by imagination. A few have discovered that reason can determine what mental images shall occupy the field of attention. These few imagine creatively, and their imagery is governed by their mental vision of the place of human personality in the cosmic order. Most people simply rationalize their uncontrolled imaginations, which are at the mercy of race-thought and casual suggestion.

The jacket is blue, which is the color attributed to water. The lunar crescents in the skirt represent the forces of sub-consciousness. The belt and trimming of the jacket suggest the combination of the circle and cross in the form of the symbol of Mars, again relating to the fact that what is apparently absolute motionless suspension of activity is really a form of intense expression of force.

The halo around the head is a suggestion that he is an embodiment of the One Light, and to carry out this suggestion the hair is white, so that it is like that of the Emperor and the Hermit. Below his head the ground is hollowed out as though by a watercourse. But all of that part of his head from the eyes to the top of the skull is actually below the surface of the soil from which trees spring. Thus we are shown that his vision and his brain functions are active <u>below the surface</u>. This, indeed, is what differentiates an adept from most people. He sees through the surface of things, and discerns the hidden laws below the illusive appearances upon which most people base their judgments and their actions.

This week use, as an exercise, the practice of checking your thoughts to see how many times the reversal of your first is more nearly in line with the teachings of Ageless Wisdom than the thought itself. Check yourself for rationalizations. One of the most common forms of this pernicious habit is the rationalizing of a desire, so that it appears to be in line with reason when it is entirely opposed to reason in reality. An overworked example, in these days of easy credit and future payments, is the desire for something that reason says you cannot afford. One, as often as not, proceeds to rationalize himself into the belief that he cannot do without the object of his desire, and then thinks that he has compiled the new dictates of reason. He has simply placed imagination above reason, and deluded himself. But there are many other forms of rationalization. Keep your eyes open for them.

TRANSFORMATION

There are so many superstitions connected with the number 13 as a symbol of bad luck and disaster that you will not be surprised to find it connected with the Tarot Key entitled "Death." But, like so many things in occultism, we shall find upon close examination that this is again a judgment founded upon appearance and superficial observation. Both the number and the title symbolize the Law of Transformation, which brings about dissolution and change. Most people have a great fear of change, not because change is usually adverse, but because its results are unknown. They fail to realize that without constant change life could not exist, and that even if it could the monotony of it would be unbearable.

13 is the number of two Hebrew words, Achad meaning <u>Unity</u> and Ahebah meaning <u>Love</u>. The significance of this is that the Unity, the One Power, from which all things proceed is also the Love Power which is the true cause of all attractions and affinities. We generally think of Love Power as chiefly concerned with reproduction, and, as a matter of fact, to Key 13 is attributed the zodiacal sign that governs the reproductive organs. But the real meaning here is that it is this same Love Power that governs dissolution and the bodily change we call death. It governs both the beginning and cessation of bodily activities. This is important, and you will do well to ponder

upon it. There are not two antagonistic powers, one making for life and other for death. There is only a SINGLE power, having twofold manifestation. Grasp of this truth is the first step toward right understanding.

Man fears death because he does not understand the meaning of this transformation. "Dissolution," says an occult maxim "is the secret of the Great Work." The dissolution of forms is imperative for growth. The breaking down of forms releases energy, which is utilized for further growth and development.

Stone disintegrates to form soil, and from soil the vegetable kingdom springs. Animals eat the vegetables, and incorporate their essences into a higher type or organization. Man eats both animal and vegetable forms, and builds chemical energy in their cells into his own body, and if he learns a secret which is available for all who have ears to hear and are willing to work, man does more than this. He liberates himself from the conditions of physical existence, and by doing so become a master of the various energies which build his organism. When he has achieved this mastery he is able to maintain his physical body for many years beyond the ordinary span of human life. Furthermore, he is able to disintegrate it at will and to reintegrate it again.

This is an amazing statement. It sounds utterly preposterous to the average person. Possibly it is expecting too much to suppose that you will accept this teaching at the present stage of your progress. But whether you accept it or not, be sure that you know what this teaching is, because when you have put yourself in a position to examine the evidence for the doctrine you will undoubtedly be fully persuaded that it is no extravagant or fanciful claim.

More than that, you will ascertain its truth at first hand by performing the experiments that will bring it about.

As a matter of fact, you are beginning those experiments now, with this instruction. You have been taught that what is necessary is for you to form the right kind of mental images. You must visualize yourself has having a body that readily responds to the power of Will which you express. Your clear image of such a changed organism, which will be a perfect and beautiful body both in function and in appearance, will have the suggestive power which sub-consciousness will accept. Then it will proceed to bring about the desired transformations. You do not need to tell it <u>how</u> to do these things, for it already knows that far better than you do. Tell it what you want accomplished and make your picture as clear and concrete as you can.

Thus will man eventually triumph over physical death. But he has already triumphed over death, because man does not die. It is impossible to present the tremendous mass of concrete evidence which is available upon this subject. Suffice it to say that it is an ascertainable fact which anyone with a little time and interest can prove to his own satisfaction. At least he can prove existence beyond the state that we call death. But Ageless Wisdom declares that man is immortal, and can never die. Though his bodies change and disintegrate a thousand times, he nevertheless remains. If this were not so the very meaning of life would be non-existent. You are approaching the time when you will <u>know</u> this to be a fact, as others who have preceded you upon the path of enlightenment know it.

The Hebrew letter Nun (pronounced "noon") means "fish" as a noun and "to grow" or "to propagate" as a verb. The fish has, for centuries, been a symbol of the Christ, which is the immortal principle in every one of us. It is only as we grow "to the measure of the fullness of the stature of Christ" that we approach anything like a comprehension of life. The moment of super-consciousness, or true Self-realization, is mystically called the "birth of the Christ child" in each individual.

The idea of a fish is closely related to the other idea of propagation, since fish are among the most prolific breeders. It has been estimated that the offspring of a single pair of codfish, if they arrived at maturity, would fill the Atlantic Ocean from shore to shore. This idea of propagation is fully intimated by the attribution of the zodiacal sign Scorpio to this Key.

Scorpio is the sign that rules the reproductive organs. Here we have the strongest kind of hint that the force used in reproduction has a great deal to do with the liberating transforming power of dissolution discussed earlier in this lesson. Do not be misled by this intimation. It has nothing to do with the pseudo-occultism that is behind the formation of many free-love cults. We are speaking here of a force. This force is ordinarily utilized in the reproduction of species. It may be utilized for much higher purposes. It may be used to change your consciousness so that you will KNOW yourself to be immortal. It may also be used so to control the metabolism of your body that you can renew it continually, or if you so desire, dissolve it instantaneously, and as instantaneously reconstitute it.

Be careful not to get any false notions into your head concerning this. We are not suggesting any abnormal restraint of the sex functions, nor any enforced celibacy. Any special instructions along this line are always forthcoming when the student is ready for them. At present you are receiving information in order that your sub-consciousness may help you to advance to the stage where you are ready for more practical work. Purity of thought and action are important, for without them you cannot advance. For the rest, the instruction you are now receiving is all that is necessary for you at this time.

Scorpio is ruled by Mars, and it is the Mars force in the human organism to which we have been referring. Mars is also the ruler of Aries, represented by Key 4, which rules the head and brain. Aries is called the day house of Mars, while Scorpio is its night house. This is a clear suggestion that when the Mars force is raised so that it energizes certain brain centers, it brings one into the daylight of enlightenment and truth.

According to modern astrology, Uranus is exalted in Scorpio. In Tarot, Uranus is typified by the Fool, which you have learned represents super-consciousness. Thus, in man, the highest expression of the Uranian influence is that which results in the state of consciousness that brings firsthand knowledge of immorality, and this state is brought about through the activity of the Power of Love.

Scorpio is the eighth sign of the zodiac, and has what astrologers sometimes term "fundamental rulership" over the eighth house of the horoscope, which is the house of death and inheritances. This one fact is sufficient to indicate the real correspondence between the 13th Key and the sign of Scorpio. But we must take the hint conveyed by the fact that death and inheritance are both represented by the eighth sign. OUR MOST PRECIOUS HERITAGE IS

THE POWER WHICH ORDINARILY MANIFESTS IT-SELF IN DEATH. The very power which, because we misunderstand it, results in sickness and death, is the power whereby we may experience perpetual health and immortality. That power is the power of life and growth to all who know and obey its law. Only to those who disobey it is it the instrument of death and destruction. Ponder the connection between that which is represented by the eighth sign of the zodiac and that which is represented by Key 8. There is a very basic and important connection between the two, which you should be at some pains to discover.

In the design, the skeleton is, on the surface, the conventional picture of the "Grim Reaper." Actually it conveys to the eye of the initiated a reminder that the bony structure of the body is the foundation of its every motion. It is because our muscles are attached to our bones that we can walk, move our hands and feet, and so on. Even the involuntary muscles have their connections with the skeleton, and could not move otherwise. Thus, what is shown here is really the basis of all of our bodily activities. Symbolically, therefore, it stands for that which is the indispensable basis of all function, of all growth and development. That something is the ONE POWER, specialized in the reproductive functions of the body. This power is the seed power, and it is to this that the conventionalized picture of a seed, placed in the upper left hand corner of the picture, refers. Note that this little seed is composed of two ovals (that is, of two zeros). From the smaller oval five rays extend to the limits of the larger one. And the two ovals are united, or really one. Here is a simple hieroglyphic of the whole process of manifestation. The inner and smaller oval is the source of radiant energy, differentiated as Ether, Fire, Air, Water, and Earth. (You will learn more about the inner meanings of these elements in later instruction.) This energy fills the space enclosed by the larger oval, which, remember is ONE WITH THE SMALL OVAL. Here we have expressed a fundamental doctrine of Ageless Wisdom, namely: <u>that an INNER POWER projects itself, or a seeming extension of IT-SELF, as SPACE, (the larger oval), and fills that space with the forms of energy whose combination constitutes the body of the universe.</u>

Write that idea into your notebook, and spend some time with it. Eventually you will come to the point where you will understand that it is a concise and accurate statement of the way the universe comes into being.

There are two details about this skeleton which will probably arrest the attention of any artist or anatomist who happens to see the picture. The figure is twisted at two points, one just above the pelvis and the other at the throat. This would be obvious if the skeleton was covered with flesh, for it would then be in a position that few contortionists could imitate. The meaning of this strange position is that the force here symbolized must be twisted or reversed, to perform its highest function.

The skeleton walks from North to South, from the darkness of ignorance to the light of perfection. He represents the framework of all progress - - the disintegration of form for the sake of releasing energy.

The handle of his scythe is in the form of a letter T, referring to the ideas represented by Key 21. The blade is in the shape of a crescent, and refers to the powers of subconsciousness of which the moon is a symbol, and thus the blade is related to Key 2. It is made of steel, which is a form of the metal assigned to Mars. Mars is also symbolized by the red background of this key.

The river flows toward the sun. It starts in the north, and makes a bend so that it flows eastward. This brings out an important part of this symbolism. Ordinarily the idea of death would be connected with a setting sun, but in this Key the sun is <u>rising</u>. This clearly indicates that the power we see as death is really the power of life. Every dissolution of form means the birth of a new one. The rising sun is particularly connected with the letter Daleth and all of the symbolism of the Empress. A little thought upon this relationship will give you deeper insight into the inner means of Key 12. Notice, in this connection, that the digits of the number 12 add up to 3. The rising sun, then refers to the dawn of higher consciousness in the state of Samadhi typified by the Hanged Man. It is this dawn of a new order of knowing which is behind the transformation shown in Key 13.

The white rose refers to the planet Uranus, and has the same meanings as that in the hand of the Fool. The small plants refer to the idea of growth, and the meanings of Key 3.

The woman's head at the left of the picture is a symbol of Understanding, for reasons that will become apparent when you take up the study of the Qabalistic Tree of Life. The man's head represents Wisdom and also Beauty.

Three hands are shown. Two are active and one is passive. The active hands represent the new works which result from the transformation indicated by this Key. The passive hand represents Yod, the Great Hand, of which we become aware in the higher order of knowing. Only one foot is shown, because this picture refers to the end of the Piscean Age, and the sign Pisces rules the feet. For this reason, also, the rising sun represents the dawn of the New Era, the Age of Aquarius.

This week give a great deal of thought to the idea of dissolution and change. Note how much it is a part of your daily life. Learn to welcome change, and overcome your fear of it. The future can hold only that which you have earned, in strict conformity with your past actions, and that which you are now engaged in creating. The one you cannot help. Face it without fretting about it. The other is in your own hands. See to it that your future is in conformity with the ideas of growth and transformation represented by this Key.

Let not the face of change be your enemy. The Bhagavad Gita says, "The wise in heart mourn neither those that live, nor those that die. Nor I, nor thou, nor any one of these, ever was not, nor ever will not be, forever and forever afterwards. All that doth live, lives always! To man's frame, as there come infancy youth and age, so come there raisings-up and laying down of other and of other life-abodes, which the wise know, and fear not." This is the philosophy of all who have wisdom and understanding, for they perceive that herein lies beauty.

VERIFICATION

The Hebrew letter Samekh (pronounced saw-mek) means, as a verb, to prop, bear up, establish, uphold, sustain. As a noun it means a tent-peg, which makes firm the tent or dwelling place. Both as a verb and a noun, its meanings are closely allied to the principle of verification which is the keynote of this lesson.

Most of the instruction you have been given thus far consists of theory. This is an essential part of your training because it is an occult maxim that the pupil must be grounded in theory before he can begin to practice. It is necessary for you to learn the terms, the alphabet, so to speak, in which your working instructions are written. Nevertheless these theories must be established and supported that is, they must be verified, before they can become a part of your working equipment. They must be tried, their temper must be tested to the utmost. APPLICATION IS THE TOUCHSTONE BY WHICH ALL KNOWLEDGE MUST BE TESTED.

This point is precisely where the teaching you are now receiving, and will receive, differs from any other systems of occult instruction. It is practical. You will be given very precise and exact directions how to apply these theories, so that you will be able to judge for yourself their value. Already you have made a start if you have faithfully carried out the exercises given with these lessons. They are made chiefly with a view to shaping your attitude towards yourself and your brothers here on earth, since a realization of the nature and true unity of all mankind is an <u>absolute essential</u> for the successful practice of magic in its true and higher forms. Also they are intended to accustom yourself to linking up the various ideas depicted by the Tarot Keys, both with each other and with your experience of life.

You must see one thing clearly in this connection, however. The foregoing does not simply mean that you will be given a set of directions that will at once enable you to practice the magical art. That art consists of the transformation of your personality, and the raising and expanding of your consciousness, until you perceive clearly and at first hand, the laws whereby you operate. The great trial and testing is a trial and testing of yourself. The Tarot represents <u>your</u> states of consciousness, the principles it depicts are the principles that govern <u>your</u> life, which emanate from the ONE IDENTITY, which is <u>your</u> innermost self.

Consequently the letter Samekh represents the trial, the probation, the purgation and purification of your personality, that it may, in time, become a fit channel for the express of the One Force, a fit Temple of the Most High, a pure and holy habitation for Spirit. Only thus does the law of Verification bring about the <u>establishment</u> or <u>foundation of the house</u> of God. As you progress with your studies and perform the practical work given to you, you are at the same time undergoing the subtle tests that prove your fitness to carry out the Great Work. See to it that you take this work seriously. You have announced yourself as a candidate for Truth. Truth will be revealed to you when you have proved yourself worthy of it. The earnestness which with you apply yourself to this preliminary instruction is your first test.

The Book of Tokens says: "Thus am I as one who testeth gold in a furnace, and this aspect of my being presenteth to the unrighteous a face of wrath. Yet by the purgation of fire do I uphold and sustain thee in every moment of thy life. Behold I am he who trieth thee with many subtle tests. Wise are thou if thou knowest that the subtle serpent of temptation is in truth the Anoited One who bringeth these to liberation." Note that this quotation refers to wrath and to a serpent. Both of these are closely connected with the letter Samekh and the underlying meaning of this Key 14.

In Key 8 we see the serpent coiled, symbolized by the letter Teth. In Key 11 we see in the letter Lamed, the serpent uncoiled and active, its head erect and its tail pointing downward and to the left. The letter Samekh shows the completion of the upward movement of the tail towards the serpent's mouth, and is therefore a reversal of the symbolism of Teth. In other works Teth shows the serpent-power as it is before it comes under control. Lamed shows it at the half-way stage of our mastery over it. Samekh shows the result of perfect control. The serpent biting its own tail has long been a symbol of eternity and of wisdom. It suggests circular movement by its shape, which establishes a connection between this Key and Key 10, to which Jupiter is attributed.

The noun for wrath in Hebrew also means "vibration." This refers to the serpent-power, which is vibratory in its activity. It is the desire-force which is the energizing principle behind all of our activities. This force can be terribly destructive when not under control, hence fully justifying the use of the word wrath in connection with it. Yet it is the power that leads to freedom, the force that always destroys limitations and impediments to free expression. It is really the tempering, harmonizing power that gets rid of discord and impurity. It is terrible to the objects of its disintegrating activity, but the wise perceive its beneficent purpose.

The number 14 represents the principle of 4 (reason) expressing itself through the agency of 1 (concentration). The verification of hypotheses arrived at by the use of reason is carried out by means of concentration. And remember again that concentration is the focusing of the <u>vibratory activity</u> at a definite point by means of attention.

The digits of 14 add to 5, The Hierophant. Thus we arrive at the conclusion that verification is also arrived at by following carefully the instruction imparted by the "still, small voice" of intuition. 5 is also the number of adaptation and desire, and it is the proper adaptation of the tremendous force of desire, through intelligent control that results in the attainment of the higher consciousness; and it is the process of adaptation that constitutes most of the tests you will be called upon to meet. The key to this idea lies in the world spelt D B Ch which has a numerical value of 14 and means "sacrifice." Nobody ever attained perfection without sacrifice. To be sure, he who knows the value of his objective feels no sense of loss in ridding himself of all encumbrances which prevent his progress, but in the earlier stages of the work one is often called upon to make decisions which appear to involve sacrifice. Experience demonstrates the error of such appearances, for it shows that every bit of intelligent elimination makes possible the expression of a greater degree of power. But at first the test is difficult to meet. Many, indeed, fail to do so, and they are the ones who are readiest to assert that there is nothing in the promises of Ageless Wisdom. Of course there is not for them. There never will be to any who have not the courage to face periods of discouragement, nor the burning zeal and fiery rebellion against the limitation and bondage of this world that enables them to carry on against all odds. You must be filled with the intense, <u>one-pointed</u> desire to demonstrate by actual experience that you are really what every one of these lessons have been declaring you are in your truest, inmost nature.

The zodiacal sign Sagittarius is attributed to Key 14. It has essentially the same meaning as the intense, one-pointed desire spoken of in the preceding paragraph. It means "archer" and it symbol is an arrow. It is a sign of the fiery triplicity, Leo and Aries being the other two. This sign is ruled by the planet Jupiter. This, of course, refers to the cyclic, rhythmic motion by which the vibratory activity manifests itself. A little meditation will reveal other reasons for this attribution.

The title, Temperance, does not refer to the meaning in common use. It is to be understood in its ancient signification as "the act of tempering, or mixing." The object of tempering is to impart strength. It does this by properly mixing the opposite forces, that is, by applying the law of Equilibration. This is clearly shown in the symbolism of Key 14.

The angel is Michael, angel of the Sun and archangel of the element of fire. He is neither male nor female (the pronoun "he" is used solely for convenience). Nor is he a person. The angle is an impersonal force. On his brow is the solar symbol, and light radiates from his head. One foot rests in the water, symbol of the cosmic mind-stuff, while the other is on land, symbol of concrete manifestation. He is the true Inner Self.

On his white robe is the Great Name IHVH written in Hebrew characters, which identifies him with the One Reality. The seven-pointed star is a figure that can only be drawn by actual experiment with a pair of compasses, for the regular heptagon from which it is derived is not only not an equal divider of the 360 degrees of a circle, but regular heptagons do not occur spontaneously in nature. Thus the seven-pointed star is a work of man, the result of his development of skill in the use of tools. This suggests that the Great Work which completes the expression of Nature's laws is an artistic adaptation of those laws by man, and not provided by their manifestation below the human level. In other words, although all human activity is a transformation of the One Energy, it is only when that Energy is transformed through human speech, thought and action that fulfillment is possible. The Great Art of the occultist requires the active agency of human personality.

The wings of the angel are fiery red with blue highlights, to indicate the fiery quality of the sign Sagittarius and its color attribution, which is blue.

The torch is a symbol of fire, and from it fall give Yods upon an eagle. The Yods refer to the five differentiations of the Life Breath into the five subtle principles of sensation. The eagle is a symbol of water, because it is connected with the watery sign Scorpio. Hence this symbolism refers to the blending of opposites and the magical equilibrium which results.

The Vase is a symbol of the element of water, which flows from it in a double wavy stream on the head of a Lion, who represents Leo and the element of fire. Thus this symbolism, while it represents the same blending of opposites as does the other activity of the angel, is nevertheless opposite in it action.

The rainbow represents the differentiation of the vibratory activity of light into color by means of water. Color is a very potent means of bringing the activity of the Life Power into our field of operation and it is my means of color that we are able to utilize the vibratory activity for the modification of external conditions. This subject will be treated more extensively in later instructions, when you will receive many exercises in its practical application.

The path rises between the twin mount peaks of Wisdom and Understanding, and ends beneath the crown of the Primal Will. This symbolism refers to the Qabalistic diagram of the Tree of Life, which is really a symbol of the Divine Man.

This week test yourself in various ways. Test yourself with regard to your own earnestness in this work and philosophy. Ask yourself such questions as: "Does my belief actually support me in the various crises of my daily existence?" "If not, what does?" "Does it promote my mental, physical and spiritual unfoldment?" "Am I any better for it?" "Is it transmuting the base metals of my personality into the gold of real attainment?" "Are my desires becoming purer, my mental processes clearer, my intuition sharpened?" "If not, am I applying myself to the work as earnestly as I feel that I should in order to give it a real testing?"

151

It cannot be too often repeated that Ageless Wisdom is not a creed, not a system of beliefs, not an escape from reality into a mirage of glittering generalities. It is not a doctrine that puts all verification of its fundamentals aside until after death. Plainly and specifically it declares that its fundamental laws have been matters of experience for men and women of other days, who are revered as leaders and teachers of mankind.

Just as plainly and specifically it avers that such experience is not miraculous, that it may be repeated, as to its fundamentals, by anyone who is willing to undertake the training of the body and mind that makes it possible. And it warns all who approach even the beginning of the Path of Attainment that it is not for cowards, not for the lukewarm, not for triflers. To the courageous, the zealous, the persevering it offers evidences that admit of no denial. It points out the way of attainment of first-hand knowledge and show how to follow that way. Nevertheless it steadfastly refuses to communicate the higher aspects of that knowledge to those who have not made ready their bodies and their minds for such communication. Or, it might be better to say, it never attempts the impossible feat of transmitting to those who are not duly prepared, anything which requires such preparation for its adequate reception and appreciation.

BONDAGE

The first thing to get into your consciousness in connection with this Tarot key is that the condition that manifests as <u>bondage</u> is an illusion, a wrong construction put upon the principle of limitation, and that therefore this principle <u>takes on the appearance</u> of the Devil. So you are warned in advance that it is necessary to look behind the grotesque and terrible appearance of this Key to discover its true meanings.

Let us start by examining the number 15. The Roman numeral is XV. X and V are the last two letters of that which we call L.V.X., or the One Force which we concentrate by acts of attention. In other words it is L.V.X. <u>minus</u> the L. L is Lamed, which means "to instruct" when used as a verb, and "ox-goad" when used as a noun. Thus L.V.X. minus L suggests the absence of the equilibrating and directive quality represented by the 11th Key. In other words the Devil is the One Force as it works in the realms of nature below man, where it is truly a fatal force working by the mathematical law of averages.

We see this law of averages working in what is known as the survival of the fittest, and we see it becoming increasingly less operative as evolution progresses. A certain poet once wrote of the Life Force, "How careful of the type it seems, how careless of the single life." In the lower forms of life countless numbers are apparently being wiped out of existence, only the strongest and most fit surviving. That is how nature perfects her types. But behold how different this is among men. Here the survival of the individual takes on increasing importance, because there is a new force in operation. Man is learning to control his environment, and he is waging a successful war against forces that cause sickness, poverty and death. Successful, that is, wherever he has developed the conscious unfoldment that enables him to bring his own superior powers into operation to control the automatic forces of nature below his own level. Slowly, but surely, he is learning to exercise the Devil. He is inserting the L in L.V. X.

In other words this picture symbolizes the false conception of the Life Power held by those who are wanting in knowledge of its real nature. There are several other points in connection with the number 15 that may help you to establish a connection between this Key and others in the series. 15 adds to 6, and you will note at first glance that this key is just the reverse of what is pictured by Key 6. Again, 15 is the extension of 5 (that is, the sum of the numbers from 0 to 5) and here you have another reversal of the pictorial symbolism. You noticed in the last lesson that Key 14 is also closely related to Key 5, so that you have here an established relation between Keys 14 and 15. See what you can make of the various relationships.

The Hebrew letter Ayin (pronounced ah-yin) means "eye." The all-seeing eye has been a symbol of deity in all parts of the world for ages past. This tells us at once that, no matter how strange the symbolism of this Key may be to unaccustomed minds, everything connected with it has something to do with certain aspects of the One Power

154

with theologians call "God." In addition Ayin means "fountain."

The eye, as the organ of vision, immediately establishes a relationship with Key 4, since an eye is the means whereby the faculty of vision is exercised. It is a commonplace that the sense of sight, important as it is, is nevertheless the commonest source of deception. Every student of elementary psychology is familiar with the phenomena of optical illusions. We all know that it is necessary to make mental adjustments to interpret correctly the things we see. A common instance is that of a man standing upon the observation platform of a train. If he believed his sense of sight he would be under the delusion that the parallel tracks over which the train had just passed had somehow become welded together as they receded into the distance. In this thought, and in those related to it, we may expect to find clues to the strange symbolism of Key 15, and the reconciliation between the surface appearance of the picture and its inner meanings.

A connecting link is provided by the second meaning of the letter Ayin. A fountain is a spring, origin, source; that which nourishes the growth of plants and makes waste places fertile. Where a fountain appears on a desert, there is a <u>renewal</u> of life activity. The "Book of Formation" says "the twenty-sixth path (on the Tree of Life) is called the Renewing Intelligence, because by it the Holy God renews all that is begun afresh in the creation of the world." <u>The renewal of the desire to escape from bondage is the beginning of freedom, and is an essential forerunner to the awakening from the dream of sense</u>. The twenty-sixth path of the Renewing Intelligence (Key 15 in the Tarot) connects the Sphere of Splendor with the Sphere of

Beauty on the path of return. Thus it becomes clear that, in spite of its appearance, the Devil has its roots in Splendor, and the outcome is Beauty. Keep this in mind when you tend to become morbid and depressed by the appearance of Bondage. Depression is nothing but slavery to unpleasant appearances, and this is told to you most graphically by Key 15.

By this time it must have become evident to you that Key 15 represents a power which both binds and liberates. In its binding aspect it creates form. In its liberating aspect it destroys form. The zodiacal attribution is the sign Capricorn, the goat, which ruled by Saturn, the planet of limitation and restriction, and in which Mars, planet of disruption and dissolution, is exalted, or finds its highest expression. When the force symbolized by Saturn is seen and understood, it is used in the practice of concentration for the creation of a happier environment and more pleasant conditions. See how clearly this is indicated by the first column of Keys in your tableau. The exercise of concentration (Key 1) puts into operation the law of suggestion (Key 8) which results in a renewal of consciousness that releases from bondage (Key 15). When the force symbolized by Mars is brought into proper activity it brings about regeneration that dissolves the appearances of limitation.

Key 15 is also connected with the idea of Mirth. Laughter is caused by a perception of the incongruous. It is but a step to the truth that joy results from the perception of the incongruity between the appearance of limitation and bondage and the truth of the situation. This is an actual fact, for the perception of reality is an experience of the most intense bliss, far beyond, yet comparable to, the most ecstatic moments that we know in our present existence.

The title is derived from the Greek "diabolos" meaning "calumniator." In the New Testament the Devil is called the "father of lies," that is, the progenitor, originator, cause, source or principle of falsehood, deception, perversion of truth, delusion, error, fallacy, hallucination, mental disorder, and confusion. The Devil represents matter as opposed to Spirit, and in Sanskrit matter is also called Maya which means "illusion." Remember that in the Old Testament, the Devil is identified with the serpent that tempted Eve, and you have the clue to the proper interpretation of this Key. Serpent is NChSh in Hebrew, and this word has the same numerical value as MShICh, Messiah or Redeemer.

An ancient occult maxim declares that "The Devil is God inverted." This means, of course, that the Devil is the false appearance which the One Reality presents to those who observe its physical or material manifestations through the eyes of ignorance. The Life Power is the producer of physical existence and the source of physical sensations. These lead us astray until they are rightly understood.

The black background of Key 15 represents darkness, and is therefore symbolic of ignorance.

The central figure itself is that of an androgyne goat with the wings of a bat, the arms and hands of a man, and the lower extremities of an eagle. His wings refer to the fact that the Devil is called the "prince of the powers of the air." They refer to the subtle energy contained in the atmosphere, which is one of the powers directed by the practical occultist. The lower quarters refer to the sign

Scorpio, which symbolizes the potencies which must be purified and sublimated before man can be set free from the chains that bind him to earth. The arms and hands are shown in a gesture similar to that of the magician, but the uplifted right hand is open, and bears the symbol of Saturn, or limitation, on the palm. The position of the fingers is the reversal of the gesture of esotericism made by the Hierophant, so that it signifies, "What is visible, what can be grasped by the senses, is all there is." This is the basic fallacy of materialism, and it is associated with the sign of Saturn, because that error is the cause of our worst limitations. The inverted torch in the Devil's left hand burns wastefully, and gives little light. It is the light of materialism, and also that of rebellion.

The symbol of Mercury, just below the navel, refers to the activity at work in the subtle processes of digestion and assimilation, which you studied in connection with Key 9, which represents the sign Virgo ruled by Mercury. It is interesting to note, in passing, that the monster is possessed of a navel, and is therefore a human production. His red eyes refer to the exaltation of Mars in Capricorn, the meaning of the letter Ayin, and the fact that vision is ruled by the sign ruled by Mars.

The inverted pentagram between the horns of the Devil is a well known symbol of black magic, because the essence of black magic is mental inversion. It is also a symbol of the domination of Spirit by the elements, another error of materialism. Thus it is a symbol of essential falsehood, because it is never true that Spirit can be so dominated, and all appearances to the contrary are delusive. Again, the pentagram is the symbol of man; so that to reverse it is to deny the essential truth that man has power to control everything below him in the scale of creation.

This inverted star is a clue to the meaning of the whole design. Man's false notion of himself is the source of his belief in a Devil. Primitive man, afraid of his environment, imagined that every stick and stone held a malignant goblin that must be propitiated. Later on all of these little demons were merged into one big Devil, just as; on the other hand, all good spirits were merged into one God. A synthetic Devil opposed to a synthetic God: that is the picture of most men up to now. It is a small wonder that intelligent people are rejecting exoteric theology.

The pedestal is a half-cube, representing imperfect understanding of the physical world, because the cube represents that world. At the front of the pedestal is a large ring. To it are fastened the chains which bind the two smaller figures, representing the self-conscious and subconscious minds. The bondage of delusion which affects both the conscious and subconscious minds has its basis in man's erroneous interpretation of the nature of the physical universe. The horns, hoofs, and tail, with which these figures appear, intimate that delusion bestializes human consciousness.

This week put into practice the things you have learned in this lesson. Get busy on your own limitations, whatever they may be. If you are annoyed and hampered by lack of physical supply, practice <u>seeing</u> and understanding what is meant when you repeat, "From the exhaustless richless of Its limitless Substance I draw all things needful, both spiritual and material." Learn that substance is not the food you eat, the money you spend, the clothes you wear. All these are the appearances, the symbols if you will, of what Substance really is. And of that Substance you have neither more nor less than any other person. All of it is available for your use.

How about your health? Are you thinking constructively about your body, knowing that it is perfect in reality because nothing created by Spirit can be anything but perfect? Are you backing up this knowledge by giving your sub-consciousness the proper suggestions indicating that you really desire health by supplying your body with the proper food, sufficient water, plenty of air through correct breathing? If you are not, now is the time to get busy. Do not delay until tomorrow. There is no tomorrow. Now is all the time that there ever is.

Do you suffer from fits of depression? Learn to laugh at appearances. Laugh at the notion of a Devil, for the most effective weapon against error is ridicule. Laugh at the Devil and he and all of his angels will flee. And keep in the front of your mind, whenever you are beset by these false appearances that which now takes on the form of a veritable devil has its roots in Splendor, and its outcome is Beauty.

AWAKENING

We now come to the second stage of spiritual unfoldment, which is the awakening from the dream of sense – the nightmare of Bondage. The first stage, as was brought out in the last lesson, is the realization of bondage, and the first intimation that it is, after all, but a dream, an illusion.

Key 16 is, obviously, a picture of destruction. But it is important to notice that the source of the destructive power is the sun, and that the power comes forth as a flash of lightning. This is obvious symbolism of the flash of super-consciousness that constitutes the first awakening. It is the first moment of clear vision, after which no person is ever the same again. It is like the hatching of chick from an egg. Once the shell is broken, the chick can never return to the egg. It has definitely entered upon a new phase of existence, and a new and fuller life is opened before it. So is it with man. At that moment of illumination he receives an initiation, and then he belongs to a new order of things.

The Book of Tokens, in the meditation on the letter Peh (pronounced "pay") which is assigned to Key 16, says; "Verily destruction is the Foundation of existence, and the tearing-down thou seest is but the assembling of material for a greater structure." A little observation will convince you that destruction is the foundation of existence. Our entire lives are spent in creating, and then in destroying that which we have created. The food we eat, the clothes we wear, the automobiles we ride in, all are in a process of destruction from the very first moment we put them into use. In the very act of destruction itself lies all of the utility that can be extracted from them.

In the sense of spiritual unfoldment, awakening is distinctly a destructive process. All of the customary wrong thinking and wrong acting must go. The false sense of personal will, of self-action, must be destroyed. This is not a comfortable process. When a man is forced to recognize that his most cherished beliefs are false, the consequent readjustment is not easy. But this destruction is essentially a gathering of materials for a far grander structure.

The first chapter of the Gospel of St. John says, "In the beginning was the Word, and the Word was with God, and the Word was God. All things were made by It; and without It was not anything made that was made. In It was life, and the life was the light of men." This passage refers to the power which we have studied before in these lessons, and which we have learned was not only the force utilized in reproduction, integration, creation, but also the force that manifests as the opposites of those functions. Hence the Book of Tokens, in the meditation on Peh, (which means literally "the mouth as an organ of speech") states: "I am the Mouth, whence issueth the Breath of Life; I am the all-devouring one, where unto all things return."

It is this power that is active in the disintegration of the old forms of personal consciousness, the rending of the veil that hides the truth from mortal eyes. The teaching that this breaking down of form is fundamental in the process of the Life Power's self-manifestation is very important. The practical occultist has to learn that he cannot hope to reach any goal he may have set for himself without first breaking up the conditions in which he finds himself when he formulates his desire. In occultism, as in everything else, we cannot have our cake and eat it too. Before we can find release from the limitations that bind us, we must learn how to break them up.

The time to begin this process of breaking up the old limiting forms is NOW, not some time in the future. You have already made a good start. You are aware of your limitations. You are making an effort to transcend them, as is witnessed by the fact that you have made the effort to follow this instruction thus far. As you proceed in it, other practical methods of combating these limitations will be given you and things of splendor will unfold within you. Your first step is to apply the principles which Tarot represents in your daily life to build the Keys into the very structure of your being.

Right discrimination is the first step. The application of the principle represented by Key 16 to the circumstances of your daily life requires concentration. Superficial observation will not suffice. You must give attention to the meaning of your thoughts, desires, and actions. You must apply the principle of limitation to overcome limitation. This is shown by the number of this Key, 16.

The man who has learned to concentrate rarely places himself in embarrassing positions through rash and inconsidered action. He usually thinks before he acts, and then acts wisely. The planet Mars is represented by Key 16 and Mars is the planet of war and rash action in exoteric astrology. But it is also the planet of the driving force behind all successful activity. Thus we see that the way the Mars force manifests in us depends entirely upon whether

163

we control it and make use of its driving power, or whether we allow it to control us, thus inducing foolish and rash activity. This power is desire-force.

Control of desire is not repression of desire. No man without powerful desires and emotions can ever attain the higher phases of consciousness. Furthermore the Mars force can never be successfully repressed, for it will always burst loose, and when it does it is terrifically destructive. Books on psychoanalysis and abnormal psychology are full of horrible examples of the perversions and human wrecks caused by desire repression. The channels of expression of desire are, however, perfectly controllable. The force that makes a man desire to steal is the same as that which makes him desire to endow a hospital. Key 1, The Magician, contains the secret of proper control of the Mars force. Formulate your desires, using intelligent discrimination, and then bring them into manifestation by concentration. Make your mental images of the desired results sharp and clear, so that sub-consciousness receives definite suggestions with which to work. The activity of the dynamic Mars force will make your dreams come true.

Some very old versions of the 16th Key are named "The House of God." Others are called "The Fire of Heaven." Still others bear the title "The Lightning-Struck Tower," of which that on our present version is a short form.

There is a tradition that it refers to the fall of the Tower of Babel, at which human speech is said to have become confusion of tongues. Thus it is related to speech and to the letter Peh. The old bible-story indicates that it is a mistaken use of language to try to reach heaven with a structure of words. The correct use of language is to control the forces of nature by making words the tools of organized thought. When we try to use words to define the super-sensuous states which are beyond words, confusion is the inevitable result.

The lightning flash comes from a solar disc, to show that the active force at work in the picture is, in spite of the seeming destruction wrought by it, a phase of the working of the one Life Power.

The form of the lightning flash is noteworthy. It is so drawn that it represents the complete expression of the ten aspects of the Life Power that are mentioned in the Pattern on the Trestle Board. This symbolism is borrowed from a fairly well known diagram which represents the ten aspects of the Life Force in the form of a lightning flash.

In relation to the second stage of spiritual unfoldment, the lightning represents the sudden illumination or flash of inspiration that comes to us when we have faced our particular problem boldly, and have concentrated the full force of our attention upon it. Notice that the end of the flash is in the form an arrow head, which is a symbol of the letter Beth, attributed to Key 1.

The Tower itself is built of bricks, laid in twenty-two courses. Thus it represents a structure of human speech, or thought, of which the components are the letters of the alphabet, which are twenty-two Hebrew. The tower represents a structure of error and ignorance, which is at the same time a House of God. Nothing is more true than the fact that these physical personalities of ours, even though they are the Temples of God, are also structures that incorporate our false notions. The ugliness and inadequacy of our bodies, their want of grace and comeliness, are the results of false ideas and the outcome of our false words. The lighting flash of true perception always makes itself felt in the physical body, because there must be a period of physical readjustment before we can pass on to higher stages of development.

The crown which is knocked off from the tower is a symbol of will-power, because the Hebrew word Kether, meaning crown, is always anonymous with "Will." This is a false crown, however, and its nature is made plain by the four letters "M" with which is ornamented. In Hebrew M is Mem, and the numerical value of Mem multiplied by four is the same as that of the word Cain. Cain, the first murderer, is the personification of the false idea of will-power, the idea that every person has a will of his own, separate from the will-power of other persons, and separate, also from the Cosmic Will.

Right knowledge begins with a flash of perception which makes us realize that no detail of our personal experience can be separated from the total expression of the Life Power's activity. However brief this realization may be, it overthrows the notion of separate personal will, and also disrupts our mental structures based upon the thought that we are living life in perpetual antagonism to the universe and to the lives of our neighbors. This is the error that is behind every murder, and this is the error which is overthrown by even the briefest perception of the basic unity of all that exists.

The falling figures represent the two modes of personal consciousness to which we give the names of conscious and subconscious minds. The flash of inspiration represented by this key upsets all of our former notions of personal consciousness, and reverses our old ways of thinking. In this picture the figures are clothed, to indicate that their true natures are concealed.

Twenty-two Yods are shown, suspended in the Air. Ten are on one side of the tower, so disposed that they form the Cabalistic diagram of the Tree of Life. These on the other side are also symmetrically arranged. These letters really stand for the twenty-two letters of the Hebrew alphabet, because every letter is said to be some aspect of the letter Yod. Thus these letters represent the sum-total of cosmic forces, and they also represent the elements of consciousness which enter into the makeup of a human personality.

They are shown hanging, as it were, in space, in order to present symbolically the idea that none of these forces has a physical foundation. This idea is just the reverse of that suggested by the rocky, isolated peak upon which the tower is erected. The average person thinks of his life as having a physical basis, that it is sustained by food, air, water, and the various physical forces in his environment. Ageless Wisdom says just the opposite. It explicitly declares that the One Life Power is the basis of all manifestation whatsoever, physical or otherwise. It by no means denies the importance, much less the actual existence, of the physical plane. But it does declare that the physical world is the manifestation, or expression, of the powers of spiritual life. In other words it says that instead of life being supported by the conditions of the physical plane, these conditions are supported by life.

Thus, while it is undoubtedly true that certain definite physical conditions must obtain in order that certain functions of human personality may be exercised here on earth, it is not true that those conditions are the causes or the <u>support</u> of those functions. On the contrary, the cause is the Life Power itself, and it is the Life Power which manifests in the physical conditions in question. The latter are the effects, rather than the causes, of manifestation.

Devote yourself this week to a study of your desires. Most of us are beset with a veritable riot of miscellaneous desires, most of them unimportant, weak and temporal. The enlightened man is a man of comparatively few desires, but they are deep, powerful, and one-pointed. Such a man shoots straight for his mark, allowing nothing to turn him aside from his purpose. His thoughts dwell upon it, his activity is directed to its attainment.

Select your most important desires. Do not allow less important ones to interfere with them. Such small desires dissipate energy that should be utilized in important things. The reason most people never get anywhere is because of just such unconcentrated dissipation of desire-force. Better one thing well done than a dozen half-done or done badly.

This is an exceedingly difficult exercise. It may look easy on paper, but it might easily take a lifetime of effort before the desire-nature is brought under control. So don't make the mistake of slighting this lesson. Don't let it drop at the end of this week either. Practice it constantly. You are lost in occultism unless you can control your desires, because the time will come when you will have to prove such control. Remember that desire is symbolized by the lion. Unless you have learned to control him, he will eventually destroy you. So begin the practice today.

REVELATION

The third stage of spiritual unfoldment, as represented by the Tarot, is Revelation. By revelation we mean unveiling, disclosure, exposure, rather than discovery. For Key 17 tells of the operation of something above the personal level rather than the result of purely personal activity. The disclosures that are made at this stage are not perceived with the physical senses, they are not something arrived at by the reasoning mind from external observations. Quite the reverse: they are perceived only when that mind is completely stilled and the senses sealed.

The Hebrew letter Tzaddi (pronounced as written) means "fish-hook." A fish-hook is a symbol of angling. Thus it is related to our ideas of experimentation, quest and research. It is a quest for that which is not yet definitely realized, a sort of groping, a feeling one's way, "fishing" for something. What is clearly indicated here is that the fish-hook symbolizes some agency or instrumentality whereby one attempts to solve secrets or enigmas, whereby one follows a more or less faint trail leading to the solution of a mystery.

This agency, symbolized by the fish-hook, is meditation, which is the function attributed to Key 17. Patanjali defines meditation as "an unbroken flow of knowledge in a particular object" and we shall see that Key 17 carries out this definition to the letter. Meditation is close, or continued, thought. It is <u>deep reflection</u>. It is a continuous dwelling upon one <u>central</u> idea, a diving down into the depths of the mind to the ideas associated with the main thought, fishing for truth, so to speak.

You will note that such association of ideas forms the basis of Tarot practice. You will find this carried out even further when you come to study the Qabalistic correspondences later on. Keys 1, 2, and 3 symbolize the process extremely well. First the selection of some definite object, upon which attention is focused (Key 1). Then the associative process, represented by the meaning of the letter Gimel (Key 2), which result in the fertile mental imagery, the true understanding, represented by the Empress (Key 3).

The numerical value of the letter Tzaddi is 90. This is also the value of the letter name M I M (Mem) which is associated with Key 12, the Hanged Man. This indicates the probability of a cross correspondence between the two letters, and the ideas represented by them. Such a correspondence is evident even in the meanings of the letter names. For certainly a fish-hook (Tzaddi) immediately makes us think of Water (Mem). It is, in fact, an instrument for lifting fish out of water. Water, you will remember, is the Universal Sub-consciousness, the Substance from which all things exist. Follow out this idea for yourself.

In connection with Key 12 you will recall that the title, The Hanged Man, is synonymous with the "Suspended Mind" which signifies, among other things the suspension of the activity of personal consciousness as the result of profound meditation. This suspension is called Samadhi in

Sanskrit books on Yoga, and is said in those books to lead to the revelation of the highest truths.

As stated above, in meditation, by keeping the stream of consciousness flowing in relation to some special object, we gather impression after impression from that object. As a consequence of this our minds actually take the form of that object. We become more and more identified with it, and thus we become aware of the inner nature of the object. It reveals itself to us.

The object of meditation is usually a problem of some sort, and this problem is most important. Just as you must have the right kind of bait before the fish will bite, so you must have some definite object for meditation. The solution of the problems is the reason for meditation. Because it is a problem, it appears to be the adversary of the person engaged in meditation. It may look like the very Devil himself, but the practical occultist knows that this is but the first appearance, and thus he disregards it. He knows the solvent power of consciousness, and how to apply it.

The first thing to do in meditation is to silence the superficial activity of the personal consciousness. Just as the fisherman sits quietly, so must the man in meditation learn to wait patiently until the fish of thought takes the hook. The hook is always a specific question. Those who imagine that they are meditating when they sit passively, imitating a jelly-fish in their mental attitude, are sadly mistaken. For, although it is true that we do not discover truth, it is also true that our mental attitude must be one of _active_ quest. We must not be content merely to sit still in the hope of enlightenment. Sill we must be, but at the same time _intent_ upon receiving light on our problem. The right mental attitude is one of quiet, but alert, _receptivity._ In this attitude we are able to hear the voice of the Hierophant, and he will speak distinctly and very definitely.

As we become skilled in the practice of meditation, we find that about all we have to do with the disclosure of new aspects of truth is the preliminary work of selecting some specific problem as the pivot of our meditation. In old Egypt there used to be a statue of Isis, with an inscription beneath is asserting that no mortal had ever lifted her veil. This continues to be true. Yet the veil of Isis is lifted again and again for those who are duly and truly prepared to look upon her lovely presence. Man does not lift her veil. She lifts it herself. Neither does Nature deliberately hide herself from us. The veil that conceals truth is the veil of human ignorance, and that veil may be removed by the practice of meditation.

The number 17 is composed of the digits 7 and 1, where 7 represents the power that is expressed, and 1 the agency through which it is manifested. 7 refers in Tarot to The Chariot, and consequently to the receptivity which is indispensable in meditation. To succeed in meditation we must be keenly aware that the personality is the vehicle of Life Power and we must understand that the Life Power, being the Logos, or Creative Speech, finds expression in all forms. It is because that Word is actually seated in our hearts that we are able to receive its disclosures of truth. The mental attitude which is symbolized in Tarot by the Magician is the means whereby the truth so disclosed may be put into practical application. Man is, by his nature, the transformer of his environment in accordance with his perceptions of reality. He IS that, whether he applies his power wisely or unwisely. We are the magicians, projecting our own circumstances by our mental imagery. When we realize this truth about ourselves, and act upon it, we shall understand the true significance of that old saying of Francis Rabelais, "DO WHAT THOU WILT!"

The zodiacal sign Aquarius, the Water Bearer, is attributed to Key 17. Its symbol is the same as the alchemical symbol for dissolution. Thus it is directly connected with the ideas which we have considered in our study of Key 13. It is apparent that this key is closely related to Key 17, since the letter Nun means "fish." In the symbolic representation of the fixed signs of the zodiac, in the corners of Keys 10 and 21, Aquarius is the Man. Man is the great fisher for new forms of truth. Man is the possessor of that Universal Solvent, the power of human consciousness, of which we read in alchemical books. It is the most potent force at our disposal, in the solution of our problems. Meditation is the process whereby this is accomplished.

Aquarius is jointly ruled by Uranus and Saturn. These two are the first and last Keys of the Tarot Major Trumps, The Fool and The World. This is a sufficient hint that the practice of meditation will eventually bring about the answers to every question, from the most abstract to the most concrete. There are many other interesting ideas arising out of this co-rulership. See if you can follow some them out by meditating upon them.

The Title, The Star, refers directly to the Universal Light Energy which condenses itself into stars, the Reality behind their forms. And Meditation is the intentional, skilled direction of the spiral force of this energy in its course through the nervous system and the brain.

The Great Star is the Blazing Star of Masonic symbolism. It is the symbol of the Quintessence, or the fifth essence of the alchemists. This is clearly indicated by the fact that it has eight principal rays. The eight spoked wheel, seen on the dress of the Fool, and the eight-pointed star are all symbols of this same Quintessence. It is the symbol of Spirit, of the energy which is transmitted by the sun. It has also eight very short secondary rays. These rays are shown fully developed in Key 19.

The seven lesser stars are also eight-pointed to show that they are manifestations of the same Quintessence. They also represent the seven alchemical metals: Lead, Iron, Tin, Gold, Copper, Silver, and Mercury. These correspond to the seven planets: Saturn, Mars, Jupiter, Sun, Venus, Moon, and Mercury. They are the symbols of the seven interior stars, or chakras, which are centers through which the One Force operates in the human body. This is a forerunner of the teaching that you will receive in later lessons. Then you will be told much more about these centers, and will learn much about their development. For the present this is not a necessary part of your instruction. Much teaching is extant with regard to the development of these centers. A great deal of this is very dangerous, because it either teaches those who are not duly and truly prepared the secrets of how much development may be brought about, thus wrecking the unfortunate individual who practices such instruction in much the same manner that a high powered electric current would do; or else it teaches wrong methods of development which force development, and the result is the same as that of forcing open a bud before it is ready. Be very wary of practices in this direction, unless you are sufficiently advanced to be able to discriminate, and know what you are about.

The Nude woman is Isis-Urania. She represents truth, and the practice of meditation reveals truth to us without

174

disguise, hence she is nude. Her legs are bent so that each forms an angle of 90 degrees, the number of the letter Tzaddi. The weight of her body rests upon her left knee, and is supported by the earth, representing the facts of physical existence. She maintains her balance with her right leg, and her right foot rests upon the surface of the pool. This implies that in meditation something occurs which gives solidity and supporting power to the ordinarily unstable mind-stuff symbolized by water. This is what the alchemists call "the fixation of the volatile."

The two vases are the two personal modes of consciousness, self-consciousness and sub-consciousness. The ellipses on their sides symbolize the zero sign, spirit, or Akasha. Only two ellipses are shown, but there are really four, signifying the expression of Spirit in the four elements. From the vase in the right hand of the woman a stream falls which sets up a wave motion in the pool, and represents the activity of sub-consciousness set up by meditation. From the other vase a stream falls on land and divides into five parts, to represent the perfection of the five senses in meditation.

The mountain in the background is the same as the one in the 6th and 8th keys. It represents the perfection of the Great Work, which is the control of the inorganic forms of the Life Power's activity, or the "mineral work" in alchemy.

The tree represents the human organism, and particularly the nervous system and brain. The bird is an Ibis, which is a fishing bird. The Egyptians associated the ibis with Hermes, or Mercury.

This week develop the exercise that you began last week. Formulate your desires into specific problems. Give them your complete attention. Focus the spotlight of your consciousness upon them. Make every detail clear and definite. Then, with that as a basis, begin the fishing process of meditation. Do not try to think about your problem. Rather let the stream of consciousness flow past you. Observe carefully all of the ideas that develop in connection with the object of your meditation. Make every effort to keep on the subject.

Keep your object always in view. If you have any very strong impulses act upon them. Have faith in the consequences of your activity. And, above all, expect to get results. Yet do not be discouraged if you do not get them immediately. Only by persistent practice can you learn the art of meditation. But every minute you spend with it will repay you a thousand-fold in practical results.

The secret of Key 17 is found in a quotation from the meditation on Tzaddi in the <u>Book of Tokens</u>:

"Thinkest thou, O seeker for wisdom that thou bringest thyself into the Light by thine own search? Not so. I am the HOOK, cast into the waters of darkness, to bring men from their depths to the sphere of true perception. Entering that sphere, they must die to their old selves, even as fish cast upon the land must die. Yet do they die only to live again, and what before seemed life to them now weareth the aspect of death. Men think they seek Me, but it is I who seek them. No other seeker is there anywhere than Myself, and when I find Mine own, the pain of questing is at an end. The fish graspeth the hook, thinking to find food, but the fisherman is the enjoyer of the meal."

ORGANIZATION

The 18th Key symbolizes the fourth stage of spiritual unfoldment. After one has realized that the condition of bondage to appearances (Key 15) is but an illusion; when by the flash of spiritual illumination false structures of our wrong thinking and wrong acting were demolished (Key 16), then came a period of quietness, as one that comes after storm, when new relations become revealed to us through meditation (Key 17). After that begins the process of organization.

As here used, organization does not mean the association of human beings into groups or societies. It refers rather to the organization of the various parts of a single human body into a higher type of organism than that which is spontaneously provided by the general averages of ordinary evolution.

The practical application of the principles of Ageless Wisdom is aimed at a change in the human organism. Creatures in the evolutionary scale below man are incapable of any great degree of self-modification. Animals and plants brought under the influence of man may be considerably modified in a relatively short period of time, but show a tendency to revert to type when the cultural influence is removed.

The "Great Art" of practical occultism is concerned with the production of a higher, finer, more sensitive and responsive type of human being. This is not affected by eugenic measures. It is not by selection and breeding, but by the direct action of man's will and imagination upon his own vehicle of flesh and blood, that the transformation is affected.

This transformation is the outcome of the working together of universal forces, and not merely the result of personal efforts. Yet the culmination of this work requires the introduction of the personal factor. No man accomplishes the Great Work until he himself sees the principles and laws that must be applied.

This accomplishment is possible by the exercise of imagination. It is by imagination that we make our desires and aspirations clear and definite. These mental images are the patterns which we pass into the sub-consciousness, which is the body builder and the controller of function.

If our patterns are clear and definite, and we keep them intact, sub-consciousness builds a body to correspond to them. This does not mean that we can sit still, and do nothing but hold mental images, and thus produce any great change in our bodies. It does mean that when our images are vivid, they not only provide us with patterns for bodily transformation, but also impel us into courses of action which help to bring about such changes.

For example, a boy cherishes the image of being a concert pianist. This image dominates his action, so that he goes willingly through the practice that would be mere drudgery to others. The practice affects the muscular structure of his hands, arms, and legs. It brings many subtle changes in the centers of sight and hearing. It affects many other groups of nerve and muscle cells. Ultimately he becomes what he imaged, BECAUSE HE HAS BUILT

FOR HIMSELF, BY ACTION CORRESPONDING TO IMAGINATION, THE SPECIALLY CONDITIONED BODY OF A CONCERT PIANIST.

The same principle holds true in every other instance. A prize fighter is dominated by his imagery, and so is a poet. Everything that human beings achieve is accomplished through some kind of bodily activity, and each type of activity is made possible through the development of corresponding type of physical structure. This is as true of the prophet and the seer as it is of anybody else. Whatever your object in life may be, you will achieve it when you have built a physical vehicle which can transform The Life Power into particular kinds of action corresponding to your mental imagery.

The number 18 expresses the potency of the number 8, working through 1. Thus it represents the Law of Suggestion represented by Key 8, as being applied through the directive activity of Attention represented by Key 1.

In lesson 5 of this course I have hinted that subconsciousness is the body-builder, and that it is always amenable to suggestion. Throughout these lessons, too, I have repeatedly emphasized the thought that it is by conscious self-direction that all the practical work of occultism is accomplished.

In reference to the organization of a finer and more responsive physical vehicle, this self-direction is the application of a principle long ago enunciated by Lamarck, who wrote:

"The production of a new organ in an animal body results from the supervention of a new want continuing itself felt, and a new movement which this want gives birth to and encourages… Effort may be in a measure unconscious or instinctive, but must be in large measure conscious, being made with a mental purpose to produce some desirable result."

The Hebrew letter Qoph (pronounced as Kof) means "back of the Head." It alludes to the fact that some of the most important organs of the human body are in the hinder part of the skull. This part of the head houses the posterior lobes of the cerebrum and cerebellum. The posterior lobes of the cerebrum contain the sight-center, so that it is literally true that our real eyes are at the back of our heads.

Just below the posterior lobe of the cerebrum is a knot of nervous tissue called the <u>medulla oblongata</u>, which unites the brain to the spinal cord and its branches, and is thus the connecting link between the higher centers of sensation, thought, and action in the head and the subordinate centers in the body. The medulla itself is indeed a knot, presenting many intricate problems to anatomists and psychologists, some of which are probably unlikely to be solved at all by those who depend upon ordinary methods of observation.

Faulty as the ordinary methods of studying the nervous system must be, because the tissues examined under the microscope are taken from dead bodies, it has been found that the medulla governs respiration, that it regulates the movement of the heart, that it contains the principal center which controls the circulation of blood throughout the body. Besides these, it has other functions of basic importance in the maintenance of the body. Thus this knot of nerve cells at the back of the head is really what keeps us alive, for its functions are carried on without interruption even while we are asleep.

Sleep, therefore, is assigned to the letter Qoph, because what consciousness remains active in personality during sleep has its most important centers in the back of the head.

Sleep is the period of rest and recuperation, during which the waste caused by the day's operations is eliminated, and new materials are woven into the bodily structure. American Indians reckon time by "sleeps", and so for that matter, do we, for we think of a year as twelve months, or moons, so that our fundamental time-measurement has to do with night.

During sleep, moreover, the plans and thoughts we have been concerned with during the day are ripened and brought to maturity. Thus it is proverbial that night brings counsel. Many a problem has been solved subconsciously during the night. Our mental processes continue at subconscious levels, even while the cells of the upper brain are resting.

It is during sleep, again, that our aspirations and efforts are built into organic structure. What we have thought and done during the waking hours goes on influencing the body while we sleep, and this is why it is so advantageous to review each day before falling asleep. The practice enables us to appraise our conduct. We see where we have fallen short, and vigorously determine to do better the next time we find ourselves in a similar situation. We intensify the effect of all our well-doing by this mental repetition of the original actions or thoughts. And then, before composing ourselves for slumber, we once more bring before us, as clearly as we can, the image of that which is our highest and truest desire. By this means we actually build our aspirations into our flesh and blood, impressing our dominant desire upon every cell.

The title, the Moon, is a direct reference to the subconsciousness and its powers of duplications, reproduction, reflection, of the turning back of energy toward its source. In its deeper meaning the Moon symbolizes the "path of return", the return of a prodigal son to his Father's house.

An ancient esoteric maxim is plainly concealed in the symbolism of this Key. "First the stone, then the plant, then the animal, then the man." If you examine the picture closely, you will see stones at the margin of the pool. Just beyond them are the pointed leaves of a water-plant, and the vegetation continues in the field beyond. Climbing onto the path is a low form of animal life, a crustacean, and a little farther along are a dog and a wolf. Then come the towers, human structures, but the path continues beyond them.

The pool below is the same as that of the fourteenth and seventeenth Keys. It is the "great deep" of cosmic mind-stuff out of which emerges the "dry land" of physical manifestation. From it all organic life proceeds.

The crawfish is a crustacean, hard shelled. He represents, in the negative sense, selfishness, crabbedness and obstinacy, but in the good sense he represents persistence, inflexibility of purposes, determination, and tenacity of purpose. It represents also the first stages of unfoldment, wherein the student still thinks of himself as being separated from the rest of nature.

The dog and wolf. They belong to the same fundamental genus, the canine family. But the wild, dangerous wolf, inimical to man, is what is produced by nature without human adaptation and interference. The dog is the result of the modifications affected in the wolf kind by human thought. Men tame dogs, and modify their structure by cross-breeding. Thus here we have in the symbolism a specific reference to the control of body-consciousness and the development of form by human intelligence.

As I have said in my <u>Analysis of Tarot</u>, the dog is a symbol of Art, while the wolf is a symbol of Nature.

<u>The path</u> goes between these two extremes. For it is the way of balance, they way or method which neither goes too far towards artificiality nor makes the mistake of supposing that everything can be left to the ungoverned expression of natural impulses.

It progresses over undulating ground, so that it is a succession of ascents and descents. Our progress is not an unbroken upward climb. We attain one eminence after another, and after reaching every lesser peak we apparently go downhill for a time. But this is only the surface appearance. We cannot be climbing all the time. There is a periodicity, a waxing and waning, a flux and reflux. Assimilation, or taking in, must be balanced by expression, or giving out. Periods of intense effort must be followed by periods of rest.

And since the path rises over rolling ground, as one advances there comes a time when the lowest point of descent is a higher stage than the peak of a previous attainment. The one thing needful is to keep facing toward the goal. So long as we do this, we may be sure that we are progressing, even in those periods when it seems that we cannot study, that we cannot do anything but rest.

<u>The towers</u> have battlements, and form a gateway. The suggestion of the design is that each tower is connected

with the wall, and the occult interpretation I have received is that this is the wall of ordinary limits of human sensation and perception. But this is not the final boundary. There is a vast region of experience beyond it, and the way which leads into that region is open for all who will follow it.

The Moon is so drawn that it has sixteen principal and sixteen secondary rays (although in the picture some of the secondary rays near the top of the design are not clearly shown). Thus there are 32 rays, and this number 32 is, first of all, the number of paths on the Tree of Live, consisting of the ten forces that correspond to the numbers from 1 to 10, and the 22 forces that are represented by the letters of the Hebrew alphabet and Tarot Keys. Hence the rays of the Noon represent the sum-total of cosmic forces at work in human personality.

Eighteen Yods fall from the Moon onto the path. In the colored cards they are partly red and partly yellow, to intimate the combination of solar energy (yellow) with the vital forces in the blood (red). The intimation is that the powers of subconsciousness descend into the actual physical structure through the blood. The body is actually built from the elements in the blood-stream, and the chemistry of the blood-stream is controlled by subconscious mental activity, represented in this Key by the Moon.

The Way of Attainment is the Way of return. The Beyond is really the source. The height to which the path leads is that whereon the Hermit stands in Key 9.

Ancient teachers have left very clear descriptions of the Way of Attainment. They tell us it is narrow, meaning that concentration is required to follow it. More or less plainly they intimate that this is a mode of life balanced between the conditions of nature and such modifications of those conditions as are possible for art. The beginning of the way is in the realm of the familiar. It leads us, by easy stages, from the Known to the Less-Known, and from the Less-Known to the Unknown. Every Master of Life has followed this path to its goal, which is Self-recognition, or correct perception of the true I AM.

This week try to start the practice of reviewing your day's activities just before going to sleep. If you are in the habit of writing a diary, that is the best possible means of reviewing one's attainments and failures. Our attainments are just the stepping stones to the progress toward self-realization. Our failures are but warnings of what to avoid in the future. What we call "sin" is nothing but missing the mark. Never muse too much about failures, merely get the determination never to repeat the same errors. There is no excuse for that. Do not worry. Worry is the concentration on the negative side of life. If you can worry well and at length, then you possess the ability to concentrate. But is it worthwhile to concentrate on the negative side? Change the polarity of your thoughts and emotions in your daily life; impress your sub-consciousness before going to sleep with positive images. Persist in this practice and the results will not fail to manifest themselves in all directions.

REGNERATION

The fifth stage of spiritual unfoldment, as symbolized by the 19th Key, is the stage of new birth from natural humanity into spiritual humanity.

In the natural man the powers of sub-consciousness are stifled and perverted by the suggestions implanted as the result of erroneous conscious thinking. But by applying the correct conscious self-direction to his efforts to grow, a man becomes truly a new-born being, "twice-born." In this New Birth the physical body is transformed, and the method of Ageless Wisdom is concisely summarized in the injunction:

"Be ye transformed by the renewing of your mind."

From the natural man the spiritual man is born, and there is no ceremonial presentation of the process of regeneration that does not employ this symbolism of rebirth.

St. John, in the third chapter, records the conversation between Jesus and Nicodemus:

1. "There was a man of the Pharisees, named Nicodemus, a ruler of the Jews:
2. The same came to Jesus by night and said unto him, Rabbi, we know that thou art a teacher come from God: for no man can do these miracles that thou does, except God be with him.

3. Jesus answered, and said unto him, Verily, Verily, I say unto thee, <u>Except a man be born again</u>, he cannot see the kingdom of God.

4. Nicodemus said unto him, How can a man be born when is old? Can he enter the second time into his mother's womb, and be born?

5. Jesus answered, Verily, verily, I say unto thee, Except a man be born of water and of the Spirit, he cannot enter into the kingdom of God.

6. That which is born of the flesh is flesh; and that which is born of the Spirit is spirit.

7. Marvel not that I said unto thee, <u>Ye must be born again</u>."

Meditate on these words of Jesus. The New Birth is a very real process of the inner realization of true status of man. It is a degree of adeptship, that of liberation from the limitations of physical matter and circumstances. It is also a grade of conscious self-identification with the One Life. Yet it is not final. For though it is a stage wherein all material forces are under the control of the adept, who, having himself become childlike, realizes in his own person the fulfillment of the promise "A little child shall lead them;" the person who has reached this grade still feels himself to be a separate, or at least distinct, entity. This is not full liberation, but it is a higher state than any of those preceding it. It is, in particular, the stage in which all the physical forces are dominated by the will of the adept, because he is the unobstructed vehicle of the One Will which always has ruled those forces, since the beginning.

<u>The number 19</u> has a special meaning in any system of esoteric teaching derived, like Tarot, from Hebrew wis-

dom. For 19 is the number of words "Job" and "to be black."

Now, Job is the biblical type of the completion of one cycle of manifestation in a period of seeming loss and distress (i.e. sterility or desolation), out of which comes a renewal that more than compensates for all the sorrow which preceded it (i.e. fruitfulness). This is evident even on the surface of the drama; but it is pretty well understood amongst occultists that the Book of Job is one of the most important texts on spiritual alchemy, or regeneration.

The connection of the verb, "to be black," with the number 19 is also alchemical and magical. We are told that one of the final revelations of Egyptian initiation was the cryptic sentence: "Osiris is a black god."

Blackness is a symbol of obscurity, of the dark, hidden powers of that underworld ruled by the solar deity, Osiris. Black is misunderstood if it be supposed to represent nothing but evil. There is a darkness beyond the light of manifestation, as well as a darkness below it. Thus the occult meanings of the number 19 may serve to remind us that behind the appearances made visible by the light of the sun are hidden realities which only the wise perceive. What is darkness and mystery to the ignorant is the source of a seer's enlightenment and understanding.

The Hebrew letter <u>Resh</u> (pronounced Raysh) means "head." We associate the idea of beginning with the word "head", and since that which is in the beginning comes first, or takes the lead, such ideas as precedence, priority, and superiority are closely connected with this letter.

Thus we have the head of a government in its ruler, the head of a class in its brightest pupil, and the heads of speech in the principal points of argument and exposition.

Again, we speak of "head" in the sense of power, as "a full head of steam", suggesting concentrated energy. Also the ideas of completion or accomplishment are conveyed by such phrases as "to bring to a head", or "to come to a head."

In this connection it is interesting to notice that the addition of the digits of 19 is 10, and 10 may be reduced to 1. This suggests that there must be close connections between the ideas represented by Key 19 and those conveyed by the symbols of Keys 10 and 1.

Combining 9, the digit which completes the series of numeral signs, with 1, which begins that series, 19 unites the idea of the summing up of all the powers of a series of manifestations, or the completion of a cycle of activity (9) with the idea of a fresh beginning, or the initiation of a new cycle (1).

The title, The Sun, suggests the dominant symbol, which is a Sun with a human countenance. It represents the truth that the seemingly material forces of nature really are modes of a conscious energy essentially human in character and potencies. The symbol itself is the conventional alchemical representation of the day-star, but there are details in the design which are important as showing the relation of Key 19 to other cards of the series.

The Sun has eight salient or pointed rays. Thus the lines passing through these rays form the same angles as the lines within the circles on the Fool's dress, the lines that form the spokes of the Wheel of Fortune, and the lines in the greater star of Key 17. The suggestion is that one and the same power is represented by the ten circles on the Fool's garment, the Wheel, the Star, and the Sun, since the geometrical basis of all these is identical.

In Key 17 you will notice eight secondary rays of the Great Star. In Key 19 those have been expanded to form the eight curved, or wavy rays of the Sun. It is as if there has been a development of power, and the nature of that development is definitely indicated, because curved lines invariably represent feminine aspects of the Life Power.

In other words, what is manifested here is the equal development of masculine (salient) and of feminine (wavy) forms of the universal radiant energy.

Besides these larger rays there are also shown 48 beams, in groups of three, each group placed between a salient and a wavy ray. These refer to the expression of the One Force in works of integration, preservation, and disintegration. Their total number, 48, not only reduces to 12, but is also 4 x 12, so that it suggests some connection with Key 12, as well as the operation of the law symbolized by that Key in the four phases of "matter", Fire, Water, Air, and Earth.

Around the disk of the sun there are also shown a series of short lines, apparently intended to serve as mere shading. But the number of these little lines is not accidental. There are exactly 125, and 125, as the cube of the number 5 (or 5 x 5 x 5) represents the power of that number exercised in a threefold manner, or through the entire extent of the three-dimensional world. If we remember that the number 5 is represented geometrically by the pentagram, symbol of man's dominion over the elements, it will be evident that 125 conveys symbolically the extension of that dominion over and through every part of nature.

Finally, the human features in the solar orb, as in all alchemical representation representations of the Sun, are intended to show that here is a representation of a living, conscious intelligence. It is an ancient occult doctrine that all the celestial bodies are vehicles of intelligence, and the farther modern science goes in its analysis of the physical universe, the more evident does it become that this ancient notion is essentially true, even though it may be true in a subtler, finer sense than was understood by our ancient brethren. The main point is that the sun, as a synthesis of all the active forces entering into the composition of human personality, is here shown as a living force, and not as a merely mechanical or chemical energy. It is a power like unto ourselves. We have something in common with it. It enters intimately and immediately into our lives. There is a sense, indeed, in which we may say that all our personal activities are particular manifestations of solar energy. Our lives, in other words, are part of a series of transformations of energy which constitute a <u>circuit</u>. It is not merely that energy coming <u>from</u> the sun flows through our bodies and takes form in their actions. It is that energy coming from the sun, and flowing back to it again, produces all the phenomena of human existence. Thus the solar energy shines in us, and that being true, our energy shines in the sun. It is a difference of degree of radiance, but Sun and Man are lights on the same circuit of invisible spiritual energy. This is a central doctrine of Ageless Wisdom, and it has important practical consequences.

<u>The letters Yod</u> which are shown falling from the Sun (six on each side, and one in the middle, between the children), are thirteen in number so as to suggest first of all the ideas of unity, and love, inasmuch as 13 is the value of the Hebrew words Unity, and Love. They are Yods,

moreover, in order to indicate the law of response which is associated with that letter.

The sunflowers in this design are five in number. Four of the sunflowers are open. They represent the four great stages of organic development: 1. The mineral kingdom; 2. The vegetable kingdom; 3. The animal kingdom; 4. The kingdom of the natural man. The unopened sunflower is the stage of development as yet uncompleted for most people. It is the kingdom of the spiritual humanity, which goes as far beyond the natural man as the natural man goes beyond the animal.

The four sunflowers which represent the kingdoms already perfected are turned across the wall, so that they face the children, as if the children were their suns, to which they turn for light and heat. The idea intended by this symbolism is that the kingdoms of life thus represented are actually turning to, and thus expressing their dependence upon, the regenerated humanity represented by the children. But the fifth sunflower turns toward the sun above. For it and the children both symbolize the same thing. It is representative of a state of being as yet in its earlier stages of development, and at present dependent more upon the working of universal forces than any embodiment of these forces in human life. That is to say, the natural man and the three kingdoms below him are dependent upon the new-born spiritual humanity, and receive their sustenance through that spiritualized flowering of the human race. But the spiritual humanity turns only to that which is above for support.

The wall behind the children is of stone. Thus it represents forms of truth, in contrast to the forms of error typified by the bricks of the Tower in Key 16.

It is nevertheless, a wall, and it is shown with five courses, in order to indicate that it is built of materials drawn from sense-experience. Those materials are aspects of truth, or reality. On this point the teachings of Ageless Wisdom behind Tarot is most explicit. It does not deny the truth of our senses. Even though our senses do not always give us correct reports, what they do report is nevertheless a phase of truth.

But the difficulty is that most people think there are no aspects of truth besides those that we learn through the senses. And by limiting themselves to sensation they build an artificial barrier that is a bar to further progress. The wall says: "Thus far and no farther shalt thou go." But, as we shall see, Key 19 has intimations of another way.

The children are nude. Thus they repeat, in this particular, the symbolism of Key 17. In Key 17 we see Nature unveiling herself as truth. In Key 19 we see humanity so perfectly identified with that truth that it has nothing whatever to conceal. Here we may anticipate an objection. You may say, "What about the secrecy with which masters of wisdom are supposed to surround themselves?" The answer is that they do nothing of the kind. The veils that hide them from us are of our making, even as is the Veil of Isis. Our ignorance is the veil, rather than any effort of theirs to remain concealed.

The Masters are the most childlike and transparent of human beings. Their words are simple. Their statements are plain and direct. That is why they are so seldom understood.

I said a moment ago that this picture shows intimations of another way than that which is barred by the wall of man's interpretations of his sense experience. That oth-

194

er way is hinted at by the fact that both children turn their backs upon the wall. The nature of that way is further indicated by the fairy ring in which they are dancing.

These two concentric circles are known to certain occultists as symbols of the fourth dimension. The way of the spiritual man is not as the way of the natural man. The spiritual man centers himself in the inner circle of manifestation. By repeated practice he has made habitual his inner identification with the ONE IDENTITY.

Hence, in this picture, the children are shown as being of equal stature, and standing on the same level. In the natural man sub-consciousness, the feminine aspect of personality is subordinate, and subjected to the misunderstandings and misinterpretations of the masculine conscious aspect. In the spiritual man this is not so. Sub-consciousness is released from the bondage of erroneous suggestion. The powers and values of sub-consciousness are understood, and they are fully unfolded. Under the right application of the law of suggestion, subconscious habits have been established which repudiate utterly the idea that because we cannot attain to certainty, through sensation, no certainty is possible.

For this reason, indeed, the first of the Tarot Keys is named "The Fool." The certainty of freedom possessed by the spiritual man is a knowledge gained by other than sensory means. Hence the devisers of the Tarot symbolism thought out a subtle way to make this clear to the initiated.

The Way of Certainty is the Way of Non-Sense, even as St. Paul said when he declared that his teaching was "sheer folly" to the Greeks. To be sure, the esoteric Non-Sense is not to be confused with the ordinary meaning of the word nonsense. Yet, as you probably know, the esoteric approach to certainty seems like nonsense to the mass of humankind.

The little girl makes the gesture of repudiation towards the wall, thus indication that sub-consciousness has been trained to accept the Other Way. The little boy holds the palm of his hand away from the wall, in a gesture of acceptance that complements what is expressed by the gesture of the girl. He is open to receive the new light on the Open Way.

These two figures are also in a certain sense to be compared to the kneeling ministers at the feet of Hierophant, who is immediately above them in the Tarot tableau, and the hierophant himself is represent by the Sun.

This week try to understand the idea of spiritual birth, of spiritual regeneration. Reread the quotation from the third chapter of St. John. Notice Nicodemus' bewildered state of mind when he has then the words of Jesus too literally and materialistically. Ponder over such ideas as "conversion", "initiation", "being born again." Notice the ideas that come into your mind and record them in your occult diary.

By the way, are you keeping it?

REALIZATION

Key 20 shows the sixth stage of spiritual unfoldment, in which personal consciousness is on the verge of blending with the universal. At this stage the adept realizes that his personal existence is nothing but the manifestation of the relation between self-consciousness and sub-consciousness. He sees, too, that self-consciousness and sub-consciousness are not themselves personal, but modes of universal consciousness. Thus he knows that in reality his personality has no separate existence. At this stage his intellectual conviction is confirmed by fourth dimensional experience which finally blots out the delusion of separateness forever.

The number 20 has already gained special significance for you as the number of the letter Kaph, to which the 10th Key, The Wheel of Fortune, is assigned. Thus 20 is for you a mental signal of the idea of grasp, or comprehension. This idea is basic in connection with the Key we are studying in this lesson, because it is in Key 20 that we see the result of completing the cycle of realization represented by the Wheel. In the lesson on Key 10 it was pointed out that humanity at large is yet in the position of Hermanubis, and that the completion of the Great Work consists in the extension of the light of Intelligence through that segment of the Wheel which is marked with the letter Yod. In other words, when man comprehends his true nature, he sees that that nature is identical with the One Reality, the One Will of which the universe is but manifestation. Thus he says, "I have no will but to do the will of him that sent me." On the other hand, he <u>knows</u> that will. He knows it as a will to freedom, as a will to joy, as a will to health, as a will to opulence. He knows that it is a will to good, to the impartation of every good and perfect gift. He comprehends it as the will that finds expression in all activity. Here and now, he sees that will expresses no lack, no disease, no failure, no poverty. He grasps the truth that whenever appearances of evil surround us it is because we are not seeing the true relations.

For such a one, daily experience is a succession of miracles. When we begin to see the light, it is like the lightning-flash in Key 16. While it lasts, it breaks down the structures of error, and shows all existence as it really is. But then the darkness of ignorance closes in again, and we have to wait for the next flash.

In the Key numbered 20, however, there is a perpetual recognition of the limitless power of Spirit. Thus 20, read from units to 10s, does express the operation of the No-Thing through Memory, or the working of the Fool's vision through the Law of the High Priestess. Here there is a freedom from all those lapses of memory which assail us earlier in the work. Moment by moment, without cessation, we see the Truth and live it. And with this recognition there comes a new kind of consciousness. WE DO NOT SLEEP ANY MORE. Our bodies are put to rest, but we remain awake, able to function consciously in the fourth dimension, so that we literally do "serve God day and night."

This is one of the meanings of conscious immortality. I testify to my knowledge that it is a legitimate experience of normal men and women. There is no more need for being apparently unconscious eight hours out the twenty-four than there is for wearing a gas-mask in ordinary air. WE ARE IMMORTAL and whether we know it or not, we function consciously during the sleep of the body.

The greater numbers of persons, however, do not remember their nightly experiences, because they have not developed, on the physical side, the means of recording it. Once this power of remembering that experience is developed, it is possible to plan for the night's work and the recollection of it will be part of the day's activity. Until one has experienced this, it is impossible to convey in any human language the alteration it makes in all one's activities.

The Hebrew letter Shin (pronounced "sheen") means a "tooth" or "fang." In its form the letter Shin resembles three tongues of flame, rising from a fiery base. The sound of the letter, "Sh!" is an admonition to silence, understood by all men. So, but more imperative, is the sharper hiss of which this letter is also the sign in Hebrew. Thus the letter Shin corresponds by sound to the final admonition of the Masters – BE SILENT.

Serpents, everywhere recognized as symbols of wisdom, are silent, subtle creatures. Jesus told his disciples to be wise as serpents, thus emphasizing, for those who had ears to hear, the ancient doctrine of silence. Evidently, then, in beginning our study of the letter Shin, we are approaching a great wisdom, which has always been reserved, something about which silence must be kept.

Silence is not kept because the Knowers of the Secret are niggardly with their spiritual possessions. It is not kept because any higher order of beings than man imposes a prohibition forbidding speech. It is not kept because there is anything dangerous about the Secret which might lead to misuse. The one reason for the admonition to silence is thus phrased by Lao-Tze:

"The Tao which is the subject of discussion is not the true Tao." This is identical with the statement of the alchemists, which is negative, though it seems to be positive in form: "Our Matter has as many names as there are things in this world; that is why the foolish know it not."

The Great Secret simply <u>cannot</u> be told. Therefore it is folly to endeavor to tell it. The wise wastes no time, invite no misconception, expend no energy in an effort to put it into words. When they use words, it is not to tell the Secret, but to assist the seeker for illumination to become sufficiently ripe, or receptive.

On the other hand, those who know the Secret are forever telling it, not only by their words, but by their lives. Thus my correspondent says, "How strange that though I had read the same statement hundreds of times... it is only now that I perceive it." It is as when we are learning a foreign language. At first the words are just meaningless noises. After a time, we apprehend some of the meanings. If we persist in our study of the language, the day arrives when not only the dictionary definitions of the words, but all the subtle connotations and implications that never can be captured by the lexicographer, are conveyed to us <u>in the very same words</u> which meant nothing in the beginning.

So it is with these Tarot studies, where not only the written word, but the infinitely more expressive language of pictorial symbol, is used to communicate the mysteries. I must again and again remind you that through these lessons you are given the keys which will open the doors of the prison-house of ignorance, and admit you to the freedom of the True World. The language of symbol is the common speech of inhabitants of that True World. All the languages of mankind are but poor translations of it. If you ask me, as some have done: "Why not put this into plain English?" I answer that wherever plain English will convey the meaning, it is my constant endeavor to use it. But no translation from the mystery language can be adequate. You must learn that silent speech of symbols for yourself. Then you will find that you are in communication with others who know it and use it.

In the old versions of Tarot, as in ours, this Key is invariably called THE JUDGMENT. On the surface, of course, this refers to that day which theologians regard as being afar off – the day when all souls shall be judged.

This, however, is but a veil for the real meaning. Judgment is the consequence of the weighing of evidence. Hence the symbolism Justice is always represented by the scales, and in the ancient Egyptian representations of the judgment of the soul, the candidate's heart was put in the balance with the feather of truth.

Again we have the idea of estimation or measurement. One might say that the Great Secret is the answer to the question: "How much do you weigh?" That is to say, we have to see that since all that is real of us is identical with what the Emerald Tablet calls the ONE THING, our true weight must be identical with its true weight. The consciousness of totality comes in here, and it has never been better expressed than by George Burnell: "Truth is that which is; there cannot be that which is not. Therefore that which is, or Truth, must be all there is." When the weight of the heart or the central consciousness in man, corresponds to the weight of the feather of truth, then the scales of judgment are balanced.

A judgment, again, is a reasoned conclusion. The doctrine of Ageless Wisdom is a reasonable one. The sages are forever saying: "Come now, let us reason together." St. Paul, writing of the giving up of the false sense of personality, calls it a reasonable sacrifice. The Chaldean Oracles bid us "join works to sacred reason." Thus we shall find, in the symbols of Key 20, innumerable references to the number 4, which is the Tarot number particularly associated with reason.

Yet it must be observed that judgment is a conclusion. Thus, although reasoning is the process which leads to that conclusion, it is also the end of that process. In this Judgment, reasoning ceases and a new order of knowing is manifested. Old things have passed away, through the operation of the law typified in the Tarot by Key 13, which is the agency of the principle of right discrimination pictured by Key 6. There is to be no more weighing of evidence, no more discussion of pros and cons, and no more argument for and against. That is all done with, and we shall see in the picture abundant evidence that this is so.

Finally, a judgment is a decision. It has direct consequences in action. Note that word decision, and its derivation from a Latin root meaning "to cut." In this you have the same hint that is conveyed by the correspondence of the letter Shin to a Hebrew word meaning "separation."

The Judgment cuts off, forever, our connection with the false knowledge of the world. It puts an end to our limitation to three-dimensional consciousness. It terminates our sense of mortality. Thus, in the Bible promise already quoted, which is directly related to this doctrine of Judgment, observe the repetition of the words: "no more." They shall hunger NO MORE, neither thirst NO MORE, … and death shall be NO MORE; neither shall there be mourning, nor crying, nor pain, ANY MORE.

To have done with all this misery. Nothing less is the promise, and to have done with it FOREVER. Not a makeshift cure or tinkering. A devouring up of the whole unhappy brood of lies. And thus we shall see in Key 20 nothing but evidences of ecstatic happiness.

The Angel is obviously the angel Gabriel, for he carries the trumpet which summons the dead from their coffins. Gabriel is the archangel of the element Water, and he is also the archangel of the Moon. This should be remembered in connection with the number of that Key in Tarot which is assigned to the Moon.

The idea here is that the presiding power in this scene is the power of reflection, or the power of recollection. The Spirit of Life in us never forgets itself, and when the day of judgment comes, we hear its trumpet-call, proclaiming our real nature, and calling us from the death-like sleep of belief in material existence.

In the composition of our version of this Key, care has been taken to enclose the angel in a geometrical design consisting of two equal circles, exactly filling a larger circle. The angel's head is in the upper small circle, and his body is in the lower small circle. This geometrical figure is an ancient symbol of the fourth dimension.

The clouds surround the angel because the true nature of the Self is veiled by appearances, and the substance of these appearances is really the same as the stream of consciousness typified by the robe of the High Priestess. That is to say, it is the flowing of the stream of consciousness which gives rise to our ideas of time, and these ideas are what partly veil from us the true nature of the One Identity.

Twelve rays of light pierce the veil. These have technical Qabalistic meaning, for in Hebrew Wisdom the number 12 refers particularly to the name HVA, Hua, "HE," attributed to Kether, the Crown of Primal Will. The intimation here is that the light piercing the veil is the light of the true Self, called "HE," by Qabalists. Gabriel is but a personification of one aspect of that Light.

The trumpet has seven rays descending from it. It is made of gold, to signify illumination. Because it is an instrument for amplifying sound-vibration, it refers to the fact that the awakening of higher consciousness here shown is actually accomplished by certain definite sounds. These are represented by the seven little rays, which correspond to the particular sound-vibrations of the seven centers in the human organism which are also known as Chakras, as interior stars, and as alchemical metals.

The icebergs in the background refer to a certain alchemical admonition, which tells us that in order to perform the Great Work we must fix the volatile. The volatile is the stream of conscious energy, always typified as water. Its flow is what creates our delusions. If we can fix it, or make it solid by arresting the flow, we shall be released from our bondage. Thus Key 12 shows us the Hanged Man, or Suspended Mind, in connection with the element of water. The state of Samadhi, or perfect abstraction, there pictured, culminates in the Perpetual Intelligence shown in Key 20. For it arrests the flow of the stream of consciousness, and because it does this by means of abstractions having their basis in mathematics, the arrested flow of consciousness is represented as ice – as it is also in Keys 0 and 9.

The sea supports the three stone coffins, in order to intimate that the real support or basis of the appearances of physical form is really the vibration of mental energy. The sea is the great sea of the racial sub-consciousness. This is the actual substance of all things in human environment, as I have explained elsewhere. There is no difference whatever between the substance of an electron and the substance of a thought. Such is the teaching of Ageless Wisdom, and in these days it is receiving abundant confirmation from modern scientists.

The coffins are rectangular, to suggest the apparent solidity and impenetrability of three-dimensional existence. In them the figures stand at right angles to the bottoms of the coffins, to intimate, even if it is not possible actually to represent, the mathematical definition of the Fourth Dimension as that which is at right angles to all other dimensions.

The three figures represent human self-consciousness, the Man; sub-consciousness, the Woman' and their product, personality, the Child.

These three also correspond to the Egyptian triad, Osiris, Isis, and Horus. Their postures are intended to convey to the initiated, hints that each figure represents one of the three Latin letters. The woman represents, by her extended arms, the letter L. The child, by the posture of his arms, stands for the letter V. The man, in the traditional posture of Osiris risen, crosses his arms to form an X. Thus these three figures typify L.V.X, the Latin for LIGHT.

Observe that the man is in an attitude of perfectly passive adoration. In the fourth-dimensional consciousness, or Perpetual Intelligence, the self-conscious mind realizes that it does nothing whatever of itself. It is but the channel through which the higher life descends into lower levels. Its one virtue consists in what is intimated by the name of the mode of consciousness typified by the Magician. The more transparent it becomes, the less interference it makes to the free passage of the One thing. "Of myself I can do nothing" is the meaning of this posture. The "X" crosses out personal action.

The woman receives the influx of power from above. Her posture, since it suggests the letter "L" is also related to Lamed in the Hebrew alphabet, thus the Key 11, which represents Faithful Intelligence. Subconsciousness, under the governance of right reason, expresses perfect faith. An unreasonable faith is impossible, however stoutly men may affirm that their dogmas and creeds deserve the name of faith. Thus the woman represents the purification following right reasoning, the subconscious response to correct statements of reality.

The child faces toward the interior of the picture, and thus he represents insight, or the turning of the mind away from the false reports of sensation. He therefore represents by his posture the letter V, or Vau, and is thus a type of Intuition, or the Triumphant and Eternal Intelligence.

The three figures are nude, to suggest a state of perfect innocence, a state of perfect freedom from shame, that false emotion which is born of our incorrect interpretation of the real nature and function of human life. Their nudity also intimates perfect familiarity and intimacy with each other, and this is of course one of the conditions of the Perpetual Intelligence, in which the true relations between the conscious and subconscious minds, and their offspring, personality, is clearly understood.

The flesh of the figures is gray, to intimate that they have overcome all the pairs of opposites, since gray is the tint resulting from the blending of any two complements, such as white and black, red and green, blue and orange, and so on. Since the Tarot Keys that correspond to the seven centers correspond also to the pairs of opposites, here is also an intimation that in the Perpetual Intelligence there is a perfect blending of the powers, or pairs of opposites, represented by Keys 1, 2, 3, 10, 16, 19, and 21. In other words, the gray flesh of the figures indicates that the seven centers of the organism have been perfectly coordinated, even as the seven rays issuing from the trumpet hint at the same thought.

The banner on the trumpet is a perfect square, measuring 5 x 5, so that it is a magic square of 25 cells, the square of Mars. Thus it evidently refers to the activity associated in Tarot with Mars. Hence you will observe that in this Key, fire, the quality of Mars predominates. Again Key 20 is placed in the tableau beneath Key 13, representing the sign Scorpio, ruled by Mars.

Finally, the banner is a square, and the cross is, like the square, a symbol of the number 4. There are four figures in the Key: the angel, the man, the woman, and the child. There are also four principal elements in the design; the ice-bergs, the sea, the group of human figures, and the angel.

The number 4 for you represents Key 4, or the Emperor. The Emperor represents the sign Aries, ruled by Mars. He is also the symbol in Tarot of the sovereign reason, which leads to the decision or right judgment. The number of Key 20 is _four_ times five, and this brings me to the concluding point: The Perpetual Intelligence is the product of the interaction of Reason (Key 4) and Intuition (Key 5). We must reason rightly before we receive the inner teaching of intuition. Lazy minds will never hear the trumpet-call.

This week try to practice SILENCE. Speak as little as you can, keep your emotions under control, and, above all, try to steady your thoughts. Notice how much more energy you are going to conserve for the useful tasks. Continue this practice of self-control.

COSMIC CONSCIOUSNESS

The last card of the major Tarot Keys, <u>The World</u>, symbolizes Cosmic Consciousness, or Nirvana.

The central fact of this experience is that he to whom it comes has first-hand knowledge that he is identical with the One Power which is, so to say, the Pivot and the Source of the whole cosmos. He knows also that through him the governing and directing power of the universe flows out into manifestation.

Words fail to give any adequate idea of this seventh stage of spiritual unfoldment. I shall leave it to your intuition to combine the suggestions of the picture with the meaning of the letter Tau, which is assigned to this Key. Here is a picture of what you really are, and of what the cosmos really is. The universe is the Dance of Life. The inmost, immortal, central Self of you – THAT is the Eternal Dancer.

The number 21 is the sum of the numbers from 0 to 6, so that as a Key number in Tarot it suggests the completion, or extension, of the power of the principles represented by Keys 0 to 6. That is to say, what is shown in Key 21 is really the result of the perfect and balanced combination of the principles explained by the first seven Keys of Tarot.

Thus there is a close affinity between Key 21 and Key 7, for as 21 is the consequence of adding the digits from 0 to 6, so 7 <u>follows</u> 6 in the numeral series. Furthermore Saturn is the <u>seventh</u> of the ancient planets, and from this Hebrew name ShBThAI we have the word Sabbath, the day of rest or inertia, and the seventh day of the week. And in Tarot, you see the 21st Key placed in the Tableau immediately below the 14th (twice 7) Key, and the 14th immediately below Key 7.

Thus the <u>principle</u> at work in Key 21 is that which is presented by Key 7, and the secret of Key 7 is nowhere better explained that all may understand than in the following words:

"Stand aside in the coming battle, and though thou fightest be not thou the warrior.

"Look for the warrior and let him fight in thee.

"Take his orders for battle and obey them.

"Obey him not as though he were a general, but as though he were thyself, and his spoken words were the utterance of thy secret desires; for he is thyself, yet infinitely wiser and stronger than thyself. Look for him, else in the fever and hurry of the fight thou mayest pass him; and he will not know thee unless thou knowest him. If thy cry reach his listening ear then he will fight in thee and fill the dull void within. And if this is so then canst thou go through the fight cool and unwearied, standing aside and letting him battle for thee. Then it will be impossible for thee to strike one blow amiss. But if thou look not for him, if thou pass him by, then there is no safeguard for thee. Thy brain will reel, thy heart grows uncertain, and in the dust of the battlefield thy sight and senses will fail, and thou wilt not know they friends from thine enemies.

"He is thyself, yet thou art but finite and liable to error. He is eternal and is sure. He is eternal truth. When once he has entered thee and become thy warrior, he will never utterly desert thee, and at the day of the great peace he will become one with thee." -- Light on the Path. Part II: 1 - 4.

"He is thyself." The quest is for the Self. The goal is the Self. The knowledge of Self-knowledge; the power is in the infinite and eternal power of the Self. The Self is the ONE, working through the mysterious, glamorous power of reflection and duality. And all this is plainly shown in the very number 21.

The Hebrew letter Tau means "signature" or "mark," but the mark is the cross. The Egyptian Tau is said to have been a tally for measuring the depth of the Nile, also a square for measuring right angles. Among the Hebrews it was a sign of salvation (Ezekiel 1X, 4). Thus it is "a symbol of salvation from death, and of eternal life." As representing a signature, this letter implies security, guaranty, pledge, and so on. A signature is what makes all business instruments valid. It therefore indicates the final seal and witness to the completion of the Great Work of liberation.

The title, the World, suggests "world-consciousness." One who attains to this state finds himself in tune with the whole universe, and discovers that the center of conscious energy at the heart of his own life is one with the power which rules the universe. In this consciousness, the whole universe becomes the body of the I AM, and one is aware that the directive CENTER of the entire field of cosmic activity is identical with the innermost SELF.

The four corners of the Key are occupied by the same mystical figures that appear in Key 10. But here there is a difference. The face of the Bull in Key 10 is, in our version, looking toward the Lion; but in Key 21 it is turned away from the Lion, and thus also away from the central figure of the Key.

This is intentional, and follows a very ancient tradition, which is followed in all earlier versions of the Tarot.

The Bull represents the element of Earth, or that which gives form. In Key 10 this is turned toward the Lion, and toward the center of the Key, where the symbol of Spirit is at the heart of the Wheel, because the mental activity pictured in Key 10 is one which turns the mind away from form to the consideration of energy, away from body to the consideration of spirit. The comprehension of the Law of Cycles (Key 10) is an act of mental abstraction in which our attention is turned away from the forms of things to their fiery essence (the Lion).

In Key 21, on the contrary, all the emphasis is toward concrete manifestation. That is the reason for attributing Saturn to this Key. And therefore the Bull is facing away from the Lion, and away from the center of the Key, in order to indicate that the movement here shown is INTO CONCRETE MANIFESTATION.

The goal of the Great Work is not abstraction. It is demonstration, manifestation, the orderly procession of energy into suitable forms, the adornment of the Life Power with suitable garments.

For the other meanings of the four animals, see the explanations in Key 10 (Lesson 13). The general idea is that they represent the four elements, and the four letters of IHVH, so that everything shown in this design is shown as occurring WITHIN the eternal limits of the GREAT NAME.

The wreath is an ellipse. Its longer axis is exactly eight units, and its shorter axis exactly five units. Thus a rectangle which would exactly contain it would be 5 x 8, the same as the dimensions of any one of the seven sides of the Vault of Brother C.R. described in the Fama Fraternitatis.

This rectangle of 5 x 8, which has a perimeter or boundary line of 26 units (IHVH again), is known to students of dynamic symmetry as the "Rectangle of the Whirling Square," which is the basis of the logarithmic spiral, concerning which Claude Bragdon says:

"Now the generic or archetypal form of everything in the universe is naturally not other than the form of the universe itself. Our stellar universe is now thought by astronomers to be a spiral nebula; and the spiral nebulae we see in the heavens, stellar systems like our own. The geometric equivalent of the nebula form is the logarithmic spiral. This is therefore the unit form of the universe, the form of all forms."

Thus the wreath represents the NAME (IHVH) as the FUNDEMENTAL PRINCIPAL OF FORM, of which the entire cosmos is the presentation and manifestation.

This wreath is formed of twenty-two triads of leaves. Each triad corresponds to a Hebrew letter or to one of the twenty-two aspects of Intelligent Energy represented by these letters, and also by the Tarot Keys. Each mode of the Life Power has three kinds of expression: 1. Integrative; 2. Disintegrative; 3. Equilibrating. The third is the balance between the other two.

But a wreath is a work of man. Nature provides the leaves. Man weaves them into a chaplet for the victor. And at top and bottom the wreath is fastened with bands similar in form to the horizontal figure 8 over the head of the Magician. But it should be noticed that all that is visible of this band is that portion which makes a form of the letter X, which is the Hebrew Tau. This intimates that the power represented by Tau is what binds the wreath at top and bottom, and also intimates that the X form of Tau is but an imperfect representation of what is more accurately shown as the horizontal 8, figure of mathematical infinity, and symbol of the truth that OPPOSITE EFFECTS ARE PRODUCED BY IDENTICAL CAUSES.

The wreath rests on the Bull and on the Lion, because man's power of giving form (Bull) to the formless fiery Essential Energy (Lion) is what enables him to weave together the twenty-two modes of force derived from the One Energy.

But there is more than this to be said of the wreath. Its outline is the outline of the Zero symbol. The ellipse of manifestation, woven by man from the forces that play through him, is NO-THING. It has just as much power over him as he gives it, and not a whit more. It does not really bind him, when he understands what it really is. The world of the Master is a wreath of victory.

The central figure appears to be feminine, but has been so drawn that the legs have a more masculine than womanly appearance. The World-Dancer is the Celestial Androgyne. She is veiled by a purple veil which in our version of Tarot is like that in the ancient Keys - - in the form of a letter Kaph. And because Kaph is the letter represented in Tarot by Key 10, the intimation here is this: The mechanistic appearance assumed by natural phenomena is really but a veil for their true character. The cosmos seems to be system of wheels within wheels. It presents itself to our consciousness as a machine. Effect and cause seem to be rigidly and unalterably related.

THIS IS ONLY RELATIVELY TRUE. The Life Power is the author and therefore the master of the law of Cause and Consequence, as truly as of any other law. All "laws" are part and parcel of the drama of manifestation. No law binds the SELF. The World-Dancer is perfectly FREE. And that state of freedom is NOW.

Therefore the Dancer stands on nothing. She is self-supported. She herself is the PERFECT EQUILIBRIUM.

In her right hand is a spiral, turning toward the right, and in her left hand a spiral turning in the opposite direction. These spirals represent integration and disintegration. They are complements, and they are turning simultaneously.

In the picture each spiral has a definite end and a definite beginning, but this is simply a limitation due to the impossibility of picturing the infinite. You must understand each spiral as being without beginning or end.

Each spiral has exactly eleven loops, so that here is another reference to the twenty-two modes of conscious energy represented by the twenty-two letters and Tarot Keys.

Conclusion

Walt Whitman thus described his illumination:

"An intuition of the absolute balance, in time and space, of the whole of this multifariousness, this revel of fools, and incredible make-believe and general unsettledness we call <u>the world</u>; a soul-sight of that divine clue and unseen thread which holds the whole congeries of things, all history and time, and all events, however trivial, however momentous, like a leashed dog in the hand of the hunter."

Leashed, but ready to be let loose, and ready to do the hunter's bidding. For the point of the Key is that when the SELF is known, it is known as the Master of the Show of Illusion called the World. And the name of the Master is AHIH, "I AM."

This week try to realize, at least emotionally, mentally and intuitively, the significance of Cosmic Consciousness. It is essentially the realization of the ONENESS of the whole existence. Read descriptions of this state in Dr. Richard Maurice Buck's Cosmic Consciousness, Ali Nomad's book of the same title, Ouspensky's Tertium Organum, Boehme's Supersensual Life, William James' Varieties of Religious Experience, and the writing of Swami Vivekananda.

Dear Fellow-Builder:

The first section of the Tarot Instruction has put into your hands the fundamental knowledge necessary for your further progress. You have had your introduction to the Tarot. You know enough about each Key to enable you to grasp easily all the instruction that follows in the other sections of the course. Yet you need to become very much better acquainted with Tarot in order to make it serve you as it should. In the hands of experts it is a powerful instrument for self-transformation and mastery of circumstance. You will become skilled in using it by continuing with the subsequent sections of this instruction.

Do not make the mistake of trying to review the first section. You don't repeat the formula of introduction every time you meet a new acquaintance. No, you watch his behavior, every time you see him, under a different set of circumstances. You get to know him better by hearing what he says, and seeing what he does. So it is with Tarot. The best way to deepen and broaden your knowledge of it is to see it from as many different points of view as possible.

Remember that you can arrange these twenty-two Keys (using them all in each arrangement) no less than two hundred forty-four quintillion ways. The actual number of combinations is 244,342,483,843,215,680,000. There are also innumerable other groupings, of which that given on in Lesson 2, is one.

217

Every combination has its own special meaning. Every combination calls forth a particular subconscious response. Every combination brings to the surface of your mind a fresh perception of relationships between ideas and things. Thus every combination helps you to organize your mind, enables you to knit more closely the fabric of your thought.

In the following pages you will find twenty-four combinations. Use one each day, six days a week, beginning that Monday after you receive this instruction. Do not work on Sundays, except the recitation of the Pattern.

Begin by picking out the Keys selected for the day. Put them before you. Study them carefully in relation to each other. Then read aloud the meditation I have written for the combination. The meditations are in the first person, so that each is a positive auto-suggestion. Every meditation is completed by the key-sentence for the day, written in capitals. Write this on a slip of paper, and carry it with you during the day. Repeat it at least three times as the day passes.

Look at the combination of Keys at least three times before going to bed. See if it suggests any ideas to you other than those in the meditation. Make a note of them in your occult diary. Then read the meditation again, recite the Pattern, and go to sleep.

By carrying out this instruction carefully you will accomplish several desirable results. You will charge your subconsciousness daily with seeds of creative thought. You will also review the entire series of Tarot Keys, from a fresh point of view. You will begin to understand, from actual experience, what a wonderful aid the Tarot can be to living the liberated life.

After you have completed this four weeks of preparation you will be ready to take up the work of the Second Section. In every lesson of that section practical work with the Keys is the principal consideration.

The tools are now in your hands. In Section first you have been told what they are. You now begin to do the work which will enable you to be what you want to be, do what you want to do, and have everything requisite to that being and doing. From now on you are beginning to LIVE your daily life in accordance with the principles and laws represented by the Tarot Keys. You feet are firmly planted on the Way to Freedom.

FIRST DAY: Keys 0 & 1

Life limitless flows through me to complete its perfect work. The power which guides all things finds in me an open channel of expression. Receiving that power freely, I freely give it to all things and creatures in the field of existence which surrounds me. THROUGH ME LIFE ETERNAL TRANSFORMS ALL THINGS INTO ITS LIKENESS.

SECOND DAY: Keys 2 & 3

The law of truth is written in my heart: all my members are ruled by it. Through my sub-consciousness I am united to the source of all wisdom, and its light banishes every shadow of ignorance and fear, I share the perfect memory of the Universal mind, and have free access to its treasures of knowledge and wisdom. THE PEACE OF THE ETERNAL AND THE LIGHT OF ITS PRESENCE ARE WITH ME NOW.

THIRD DAY: Keys 4 & 5

The Mind that frames the worlds is ruler of my thoughts: I listen for its instruction. Through me the One Life sets its house in order, and makes known the hidden meaning of its ways and works. It arms me against all appearances of hostility, and by its revelation of truth I meet and solve the problems of this day. DIVINE REASON GUIDES MY THOUGHT AND DIRECTS MY ACTION THROUGH THE INSTRUCTION OF THE VOICE OF INTUITION.

FOURTH DAY: Keys 6 & 7

The healing radiance of the One Life descends upon me: it fills the field of my personal existence with the heavenly influences of strength and peace. All the forces of my being are rightly dispensed, for I yield myself utterly to the sure guidance of the One Will which governs all things. I see things in their true relationships and proportions, and my words, expressing this clear vision, are words of power. THIS DAY I THINK AND ACT WITH TRUE DISCRIMINATION, FOR MY PERSONALITY IS THE VEHICLE OF THE LORD OF LIFE.

FIFTH DAY: Keys 8 & 9

My strength is established, and I rejoice, for I am one with the single source of all power. Nothing is, or can be, my antagonist, for I am a perfectly responsive instrument through which the Primal Will finds free expression. All the subtle vibrations of cosmic energy work together for my liberation, and even now the Hand of the Eternal leads me step by step along the way to freedom. ALL THE

FORCES OF THE UNIVERSE ARE OBEDIENT SERVANTS TO THE ONE IDENTITY, MY OWN TRUE SELF.

SIXTH DAY: Keys 10 & 11

One power spins electrons around the nucleus of an atom, whirls planets around the suns, expresses itself in all the cycles of universal activity, yet remains ever itself, and perpetually maintains its equilibrium. The sum-total of the revolutions of the great universe, including all activities, is inseparable from the successive transformations of energy which constitute my life-history. Every detail of my daily experience is some part of a cosmic cycle of transformation and adjustment. THE WHIRLING FORCE WHICH MOVES THE WORLDS IS THE MOTIVE POWER IN ALL MY PERSONAL ACTIVITIES.

SEVENTH DAY:

Use the Pattern only today.

EIGHTH DAY: Keys 12 & 13

I do nothing of myself: these thoughts and words and deeds are but the ripening of the seeds of past activities. Every phase of my personal existence depends utterly upon the motion of the One Life; therefore I am free from fate, free from accident, free even from death, since what I truly am can suffer neither decay nor change. By knowledge of the truth I reverse all former pain-bearing errors, and as the darkness of ignorance passes away, the light of a new understanding is dawning in my heart. I SUSPEND

221

THE ERROR OF PERSONAL ACTION, AND THUS DISSOLVE THE LIE OF SEPARATION.

NINTH DAY: Keys 14 & 15

Recognizing every detail of my life-experience to be the operation of the One Life, I perceive that every appearance of adversity must be in truth but a mask worn by that same Life, to test my power to know it, even through the most forbidding veils. Like a wise teacher the One Life sends me problems that in the solutions I may receive renewed proofs that nothing whatsoever may be excluded from the perfect order of the Great Plan. THAT WHICH WAS AND IS AND WILL BE IS THE ONLY REALITY: THIS DAY I SEE THE FACE OF THE BELOVED BEHIND EVERY MASK OF ADVERSITY.

TENTH DAY: Keys 16 & 17

I am awakened from the nightmare of delusion, and know the truth that God, Man and Universe are but three names for the One Identity reveals itself to me. Fear makes men build themselves prisons which they call places of safety, but he who has seen the vision of the Beloved has no room in his heart for fear. I NEED NO BARRIERS OF PROTECTION, FOR THE LIFE OF ALL CREATURES IS MY TRUEST FRIEND.

ELEVENTH DAY: Keys 18 & 19

My feet are set upon the path of liberation, which shall lead me far from the limits of the world of sense-illusion. I follow the Way of Return, as a child turns its face homeward at the end of the day. I do not see the end of the road, for it goes beyond the boundaries of my present vision; but I know the sun shines there, and that joy is there, for I have heard the messages of encouragement sent back by those who have gone on ahead. MY EYES ARE TURNED TOWARD THE HEIGHTS: I PRESS ON TOWARD THE NEW LIFE OF A NEW DAY.

TWELFTH DAY: Keys 20 & 21

The life of the heavens is manifested by me, here on earth. The fire of right knowledge burns away the bonds of illusion; the light of right understanding transforms the face of the world. Through me the Perpetual Intelligence which governs all things administers its perfect law. MINE IS THE LIFE ETERNAL, TREADING THE JOYOUS MEASURES OF THE DANCE OF MANI-FESTATION.

THIRTEENTH DAY: Keys 0, 1, 2

This "self-consciousness" of mine is the means whereby the cultural power of the One Life may be directed to the field of subconscious activity. Its primary function is that of alert attention. As I watch closely the sequence of this day's events, their true meaning will be transmitted to my sub-consciousness, there to germinate in forms of right knowledge and right desire. TODAY I AM ON THE ALERT.

FOURTEENTH DAY:

Use the Pattern only today.

FIFTEENTH DAY: Keys 3, 4, 5

My personal world is <u>as I see it</u>. If the images arising from my sub-consciousness are consequences of my faulty perceptions of other days, the new knowledge I have gained will help me to detect and destroy them. By being thus ever on the watch I shall set my world in order. Thus, too, shall I make ready to hear the Voice of Intuition, which will enable me to solve my problems when I am confronted with appearances of disorder which my reasoning will not set straight. I SEE THINGS AS THEY ARE.

SIXTEENTH DAY: Keys 6, 7, 8

Consciousness and sub-consciousness work together in my life as harmoniously balanced counterparts. I yield my whole personality to the directive and protective influx of the One Life. All the mighty forces of vibration below the level of my self-consciousness are purified and adjusted by the Master Power of which I am the receptive vehicle. HARMONY, PEACE AND STRENGTH ARE MINE.

SEVENTEENTH DAY: Keys 9, 10, 11

The Will of the Eternal guides me to perfect union with the One Identity. Every detail of my daily experience is in truth a revolution of that Will through the cycles of its expression. What I do now is inseparable from the cosmic sequences of manifestation which establish the reign of justice throughout creation. THE ONE POWER, MANIFESTING THE PERFECT ORDER OF THE UN-

IVERSE, KEEPS ME POISED THROUGH ALL CHANGES.

EIGHTEENTH DAY: Keys 12, 13, 14

Every detail of my personal activity is really some part of the operation of the cosmic life. Today I reap the fruits of the thoughts and words and deeds of other days, and pass on to better things. I am guided, moment by moment, by the overshadowing presence of the ONE IDENTITY. MY PERSONALITY DOES NOTHING OF ITSELF, PASSING FROM STAGE TO STAGE OF ITS GROWTH BY THE POWER OF THE ONE LIFE, TOWARD THE GOAL OF FREEDOM.

NINETEENTH DAY: Keys 15, 16, 17

Every appearance of adversity and antagonism is but an evidence of my faulty vision. Let me be freed today from the delusions of separateness. Let my eyes be opened to the radiant splendor of the Truth of Being. I REJOICE IN MY PROBLEMS, FOR THEY STIMULATE MY CONSCIOUSNESS TO OVERCOME ERROR, THAT I MAY SEE THE BEAUTY OF THE DIVINE PERFECTION.

TWENTIETH DAY: Keys 18, 19, 20

Every cell of my body is animated by the cosmic urge to freedom. I turn my back upon the limitations of the past, and face courageously toward the new way which opens before me. I live now in eternity. MY VERY FLESH IS THE SEED-GROUND FOR A NEW LIFE, FREE FROM THE BONDAGE OF TIME AND SPACE.

TWENTY-FIRST DAY:

Use the Pattern only today.

TWENTY-SECOND DAY: Keys 1, 2, 3

I am not deceived by the manifold illusions of sensation. For I continually remember that all these appearances are but reflections of a single Reality. By its power of deductive reasoning, my sub-consciousness develops the seed of right observation into a rich harvest of wisdom. ALERT AND CONCENTRATED, I SEE CLEARLY, MAKE CLEAR AND DEFINITE MEMORY RECORDS OF EXPERIENCE, AND THUS COLLECT MATERIAL FOR THE GROWTH OF RIGHT UNDERSTANDING.

TWENTY-THIRD DAY: Keys 4, 5, 6

The empire of Universal Order includes the little province of my personal existence. All experience teaches me the perfection of the Great Plan. Consciously and subconsciously I respond to the perfect Wisdom which rules all creation. THROUGH ME THE ONE LIFE ESTABLISHES ORDER, REVEALS THE SIGNIFICANCE OF EVERY PHASE OF MANIFESTATION, RIGHTLY DISPOSES OF ALL THINGS.

TWENTY-FOURTH DAY: Keys 7, 8, 9

The One Life lives through me. Its vital fire pervades my being. Its unfailing Will sustains me continually. THE MASTER PRINCIPLE OF THE UNIVERSE, DWEL-

LING IN MY HEART, PURIFIES AND PERFECTS ME
TO THE HEIGHTS OF UNION WITH ITSELF.

TWENTY-FIFTH DAY: Keys 10, 11, 12

The revolutions of circumstance in the outer world are manifestations of the One Power seated in my heart. That Power maintains its perfect equilibrium through all these sequences of cause and effect. My personal activities have no existence apart from that Power, because all manifestation depends upon it. THE WHEEL OF LIFE REVOLVES AROUND THE CENTER OF PURE SPIRIT, PRESENT EVERYWHERE AND THEREFORE CENTERED IN MY HEART. THIS UNMOVED MOVER OF ALL CREATION IS MY IS UNFAILING STAY.

TWENTY-SIXTH DAY: Keys 13, 14, 15

Out of the darkness of the unknown comes the power which sets me free. The way of liberation stands open before me. I face this day's tests with a joyful heart. AS I DIE TO THE OLD PERSONALITY, FULL OF DELUSION, AND FACE THE UNKNOWN FUTURE BRAVELY, CONFIDENT OF SUPPLY FOR EVERY NEED, MY FEARS DISSOLVE IN THE CLEAR SUNLIGHT OF RIGHT UNDERSTANDING.

TWENTY-SEVENTH DAY: Keys 16, 17, 18

Let others imprison themselves in their towers of false knowledge: I will be free. Let others dread the workings of our Mother Nature: I will love all her ways. Let others be the servants of the body which they hate, because they are its slaves: I will make it my servant, and love it for its faithful responsiveness. RENOUNCING EVERY ERROR, I SEEK TO GROW IN KNOWLEDGE OF TRUTH, AND WORK TO MAKE MY FLESH AND BLOOD THE GLORIOUS EMBODIMENT OF LIFE ETERNAL.

TWENTY-EIGHTH DAY:

Use the Pattern only today.

When you have finished these exercises you will be rightly prepared for the intensely interesting and practical lessons of Section Second. If you have not yet sent in your subscription, do it now, so that there may be no break in your work after the completion of this series of practices.

ROSICRUCIAN ORDER OF THE GOLDEN DAWN

The Rosicrucian Order of the Golden Dawn operates as an outer expression of the philosophy, objective, and practical work found in the public declarations of the Rosicrucians in the Fama and Confessio, which were published in Germany in 1610 and 1615, respectively. In these documents, the authors declare a method and society involved in the transformation of man into a compassionate, socially aware individual, committed to the service of the Brotherhood of Humanity, and the extension of the true gifts of Mankind. Compassion (R.C., "roke", Hebrew for "tenderness") is the true mark of a Rosicrucian and the motivation of our Work.

In 1888, three high ranking Adepts of the Western Mystery Tradition formed the Hermetic Order of the Golden Dawn (H.O.G.D.). Around the turn of the century, a series of events culminated in the revolt of the Adepti of the H.O.G.D. and the consequent expulsion of MacGregor Mathers who at this time was the only remaining founder. The remaining Adepti continued the Order as the "Stella Matutina" (with the support of one of the founders, William Wynn Wescott) and MacGregor Mathers went on to reformulate the Order as the "Rosicrucian Order of the Alpha et Omega". Much of this has been documented by R.A. Gilbert and Darcy Kuntz and we direct those interested in such to the published works of these gentlemen.

It is sufficient to state for the purpose of this introduction, the original stream of the H.O.G.D. and its two branches have continued to this day. The Founders of the Rosicrucian Order of the Golden Dawn (R.O.G.D.), have been personally trained by the leaders of each in fully operating Esoteric Orders. The Work of the R.O.G.D. includes and expands upon the work of the three encompassing the highest grades of the Golden Dawn and Rosicrucian Tradition. The R.O.G.D. acknowledges Apostolic Succession and strongly endorses the value of Lineage and its importance within our Tradition. Each grade of the R.O.G.D. has been received in proper form by those who have received such all the way to the original Founders of the H.O.G.D. and beyond.

All candidates for Initiation into the R.O.G.D. must complete a six-month Probationary Membership. The R.O.G.D., as a vehicle for the True and Invisible Rosicrucian Order, offers this service "gratis", that is, we offer it as a genuine gift and we do not ask anything in return, monetary or otherwise. The only condition is to turn in each month's record before we send out the next lesson.

Currently we offer Initiation at our Mother Temple located in Southern California. Membership requires a monthly attendance and a few additional times a year for grade work. The astral component of our rituals is a critical aspect, but the candidate must be physically present at our Initiation and Grade Rituals.

Please visit our web site at www.rogd.org

Printed in the United States
219082BV00001B/65/P